Here is what parents and professionals are saying about Dr. Karen Crum and PERSEVERING PARENT:

"I just couldn't put the book down! I loved it ALL and know it will minister to many. *Persevering Parent* reminded me that I am not alone as a special-needs parent—it left me feeling affirmed, inspired and hopeful. Stories of Dr. Crum's own personal journey as well as those from other families will have you crying and cheering. The biblical truth and reflection questions within each chapter will strengthen your faith in God who gives hope in all circumstances. This book is truly a gift for all readers and especially for parents with a special-needs child. I have no doubt you will feel the 'written hug'!"

—Cathy Stenzel
parent of child with autism, educator

"Dr. Karen Crum, in her book *Persevering Parent,* has done something remarkable and rare. Not only does she invite you into the difficult, hectic, exhausting world of a special-needs parent, she also invites you into the struggles of her heart and her faith. This book is an honest lived experience of the journey towards acceptance, wisdom and hope through extremely difficult times. The faith-based study guides allow you to experience your own journey toward being a hopeful, life-giving parent. A must-read for all parents."

—Kathryn Ranken
marriage and family therapist, special education teacher

"Families of children with special needs inevitably feel alone and discouraged. I know in my own journey of parenting I often cry out for help and strength. Dr. Crum not only validates the struggles of families in a way that gives voice to their challenges and pain but more importantly gives real hope. Having walked in the shoes of parents who have come to the end of themselves, this is an honest perspective of the difficult realities that are faced. But there are treasures found in darkness (Isaiah 45:3) and Dr. Crum leads us on a remarkable journey to see the beauty and gifts God gives in the midst of the pilgrimage of parenting our children and finding peace. There are few things more powerful than personal testimony that reveals an unembellished view into the questions and fears of our heart yet emerges from great testing with hope and joy. This book will encourage you and constantly drive you to the source of hope and strength. It invites you to find your own story of victory in a powerful way."

—Rick Caldwell
minister, Little Country Church; father of a child with special needs

"As the parent of a child with special needs, I have read many books and articles to equip myself for the challenges of parenting. As I cracked open the cover of Dr. Karen Crum's *Persevering Parent,* unexpected tears of relief streamed down my face as I began to read the table of contents—*finally someone understands my journey.* Page after page replaced isolation and fear with encouragement and hope, turning me in the direction of my Maker, the source of all provision and healing. This book is a must-read for anyone who has every parented a child with social, emotional or behavioral challenges. We have read and discussed *Persevering Parent* chapter by chapter in our parent support group. The easy-to-read format and discussion questions within each chapter encourage meaningful discussion and personal growth. Thank you Dr. Crum for this important work."

—**Rachelle Busby**
parent support group leader and mother of a child with autism

"In *Persevering Parent,* Dr. Crum captures the deeply personal struggles that parents of children with neurobiological disorders often bear alone or in silence. Using real-life experiences of families, the author beautifully combines humor, introspection, and God's word to help parents better understand and appreciate the "blessings of living in God's truth." This book is practical, with solid advice to help any parent. It is especially comforting for the parent who loves but must adjust to and repeatedly grieve for their child with neurobiological impairments. Dr. Crum succinctly and poignantly reminds us that we are human, forgiven, offered hope, and most importantly, doing God's work.

I love this book. It is presented in an easy-to-read, user-friendly workbook style that can be used individually or in a support group setting. I am excited about using it as a teaching guide for my classes with foster and adoptive parents."

—**Sheri Wiggins, M.S.W.**
Program Director, Shasta College Foster and Kinship Care
Education Program; mother of four children—three with neurobiological illnesses.

"This book is excellent! As a psychiatrist who specializes in this field of work, I have longed for such a book that would offer hope and tangible strategies for parents to understand, cope, and enter the world of their challenged child. Thanks be to God for his gifting of insight and knowledge to Dr. Crum."

—**Lynn Pappas, M.D.**
psychiatrist

"I loved *Persevering Parent* and could not put it down until I read every word. It is a must-read for any and every parent. With a comfortable and easy-to-read style, Dr. Crum expertly guides parents to find hope, strength and happy endings through faith in God and in His word. Because our role as a parent is never-ending, even parents of adults will find strength and inspiration within the pages of Persevering Parent. I recommend that you read it—you will be engaged and encouraged from beginning to end."

—Kandis Lighthall
Educational Specialist in autism and developmental disabilities,
author of Homeschooling the Child with Autism.

"When a parent is entrusted with the care of a child who has neurobiological illness the responsibilities and challenges can be overwhelming. In *Persevering Parent,* Karen shares personal struggles common to special-needs families and counters them with strength from her Christian faith. She provides compassion, understanding, insight, guidance and hope to parents and families. As parent to an adult child with schizoaffective disorder and a sibling of twin sisters with bipolar disorder, I was emotionally and spiritually moved by this book. It confirms to me how fragile we are in our human experiences and yet how intimately our faith and love for God and each other sustains us."

—Dana Turgal
President - National Alliance on Mental Illness (NAMI)
Shasta County, California chapter

Parents of children with special needs hunger for hope and yearn for strength to meet the demands of stressful and often disheartening days. As a mother long-traveling this road, I appreciate the validation and comfort contained in *Persevering Parent.* This work offers encouragement for those at the beginning- or any point along- such a parenting journey. In this unique and important book, with empathy and compassion, Dr. Crum, a fellow-traveler, points readers to our ultimate source of hope- our loving and sovereign Creator."

—Betty Newcome
parent of children with bipolar and autism, teacher

"I am so proud of my sister in Christ for the beautiful way she shares her life experiences in *Persevering Parent*—including her fears, struggles and break-throughs. Karen's insight into the lives of children with special needs and their families is profound. I have full confidence that God will use this book to bring healing, wholeness and "new life" to families facing similar issues. From the first page to the last, Dr. Crum is refreshingly honest and brings glory to our God and King. This can only come from a deep and intimate relationship with the Creator. I recommend this book to anyone—not only to parents of children with social, emotional or behavioral challenges. All of us need to hear the wisdom gained from Karen's life experiences."

—Gracyne Gibson
Chaplain, Youth for Christ; Evangelistic Minister, Anderson Church of Christ

Persevering Parent is an honest, real-life account of the peaks and valleys of parenthood. The writing is grounded in scripture, full of godly wisdom and sure to impart hope, direction and encouragement to the reader. I am confident this book will bless all parents, especially those with special-needs kids".

—Phillip Baker
Minister, Anderson Church of Christ

PERSEVERING
PARENT

PERSEVERING PARENT

Finding Strength
to Raise Your Child
with
Social, Emotional
or Behavioral Challenges

DR. KAREN CRUM

All inquiries, including those for permissions, special events and bulk purchase discounts, should be directed to the author at www.PerseveringParent.com.

Unless otherwise noted, all Scriptures are taken from the *Holy Bible, New International Version®, NIV®*. Copyright © 1973, 1978, 1984 by Biblica, Inc.™ Used by permission of Zondervan. All rights reserved worldwide. www.zondervan.com

Scripture references marked KJV are taken from the *King James Version* of the Bible. *Authorized King James Version.*

Scripture references marked NKJV are taken from the *New King James Version*. Copyright © 1982 by Thomas Nelson, Inc. Used by permission. All rights reserved.

ISBN 10: 149736759X
ISBN 13: 978-1497367593
Library of Congress Catalog Card Number: 2012906030

Create Space
Charleston, SC

Order direct from www.PerseveringParent.com or www.CreateSpace.com/4718777. Also available through Amazon.com and other major distributors.

This book is dedicated to the "changer of names"—to the God of the Bible, who can change a person's purpose in life so drastically that he or she needs a new identity. Children with neurological challenges and their parents sometimes need a new lease on life, and God is here to change their lives in miraculous ways. My prayer is that the families who read this book will experience the transforming power of God in a very personal way.

I will change your name
Your name will no longer be …
Wounded,
Outcast,
Lonely and Afraid
I will change your name
Your new name will be …
Confidence, Joyfulness, Overcoming One
Faithfulness, Friend of God
One Who Seeks My Face

—D. J. Butler

CONTENTS

ACKNOWLEDGMENTS

I am grateful to many people who contributed to the completion of this book. First, I would like to thank friends and fellow parents who, over the years, have shared their stories and thoughts with me about raising a child with social, emotional, or behavioral challenges. Thank you to Debbie, Cathy, Monica, Gina, Erin, Michelle, Diane, Brook, Kat, Betty, and others whose names are not mentioned here. Your understanding, friendship, and very presence in my life have been a gift.

Much love and thanks is deserved by those who have helped me grow spiritually as an adult and as a mother. I am especially indebted to Jim and Mary Rackley, Teresa Kimbel, Joanne Wells, and Gracyne Gibson, whose Christlike examples and teaching have been particularly influential in my life.

To my first editor, Candace Brown Dyer, thank you for your talent and willingness to take on this project. You blessed me more than you know with your technical help and encouragement when I first began writing. Your belief in the importance of this book inspired me to keep going when fatigue set in.

I would also like to acknowledge members of the Neighborhood Church special-needs parent support group, who were the first to read and use this book in their parenting fellowship. Thank you Rachelle, Krystal, Penny, Timothy, Michelle, Paul, Dana, Jennifer, Karissa, Barbie, Ruthi, Connie, and Renee for your valuable input and insights. You made me laugh, cry, and thank God once again for His provisions of friendship and encouragement.

To my family: Thank you, Bryan, my wonderful husband, who supported the writing of this book in numerous ways. As a husband and father, your stability and cheer continually bring joy into my life. You have loved your family well—and we love you back!

Much appreciation and affection goes to my parents, Robert and Loretta Estu, who introduced me to God and raised me to persevere through challenges. Your contributions to my life and, indirectly, to this book, are immeasurable.

Finally, I am indebted to my children, Katie and Madeline, for allowing me to share our family experiences in order to encourage other parents and families. I am especially grateful to Katie, whose most difficult struggles are described in this book. I am awed by your courage and maturity in allowing me to share so others will benefit. You are loved, valued, forgiven—strong, wise, and wonderful.

To both Katie and Madeline, we've endured some difficult times, but God has used them for good. Look how far we've come and how much fun we've had along the way—in spite of everything! As you emerge into young adulthood, I am happy to say I enjoy you as my friends as well as my children. You are a gift to me and an inspiration to others. Trust God to strengthen you and bring you continually forward—and listen carefully as He whispers your names.

HOW TO USE THIS BOOK

The purpose of *Persevering Parent* is to explore the tough questions that arise from raising a child who has social, emotional, or behavioral challenges and to provide you, the caregiver, with spiritual and practical encouragement along the way. You can read this book on your own to gain insight and comfort when you are feeling alone or misunderstood, as you experience grief, or as you encounter questions and concerns about raising your child. During the moments that you do not have immediate support from someone who understands, I hope this book will serve as a kind of "written hug."

This book can also be used as a study guide for faith-based support groups for parents of special-needs children. If used in this setting, I suggest you read one chapter before attending each group meeting. As you read, answer the reflection and discussion questions integrated within each chapter. Your support group will serve as a great forum in which to share your answers with other parents who understand your circumstances. The practical and spiritual encouragement that you will likely gain from this fellowship will be invaluable.

For further suggestions on using this book in a support-group format, see the appendix, "Suggestions for Persevering Parent Support Groups."

INTRODUCTION

The first time my preschooler with autism hurt her younger sister, she was only four. The report came from the preschool teacher. The two of them had been on the playground, and Katie had thrown a rock at Madeline, striking her head. While the physical damage was not serious, it had caused a flood of tears from my two-year-old. I was shocked, concerned, and disappointed, but as I scolded Katie and comforted Madeline, I had no way of knowing this event would mark the beginning of many similar outbursts. The years following this incident would be characterized by Katie's anxiety, grief, refusal to cooperate, and periods of aggression. As her parents, my husband and I vacillated between feelings of sadness, concern, anger, hope, frustration, encouragement, and desperation—sometimes simultaneously.

The good news is that although the autism and some of the challenges related to that condition continue, Katie, who is now a young adult, is no longer chronically anxious, sad, or aggressive. She has developed into a bright, sensitive, and friendly young woman. She is a high school graduate, is working a part-time job, and has attended community college. She received her driver's license and now drives herself to work, church, appointments, and a variety of other activities. Although there are ups and downs, she is relatively happy. Life is good. It's a state we don't take for granted, as her life has not always been this simple. Although my husband and I realize there are many unknowns in the years ahead, we have seen other families follow a similar path and witnessed their children move from great difficulty to relative stability.

These positive outcomes have been accomplished only through a fair amount of weeping and gnashing of teeth on the part of all immediate family members. Raising a child with a neurobiological and/or behavioral disability is a difficult task. Even if the behaviors are not outwardly disruptive, as with a child who is depressed, withdrawn, or anxious, the challenges are many. The first few years after identifying a problem were daunting for Bryan and me as we sought a diagnosis, gained appropriate intervention, and worked through our shock and grief. During the ensuing years, many questions surfaced about the future. How would our child function physically, socially, emotionally, academically, and spiritually? Would we be able to help her? Would others help her or hurt her? What if our worst fears came true? Would she be independent one day? Would we ever be happy again?

Dealing with these social, emotional, and behavioral problems presented additional challenges for us as Christian parents, as we were supposed to be raising our children to demonstrate Christian behavior. If Katie was disruptive, it could stimulate the judgment of others. If she or her sister was anxious and not fully engaged in activities, that behavior could also be misinterpreted. While these behaviors often resulted from neurological dysregulation more than personal choice, the consequences were often identical. We would do most anything to help our child, but we struggled with anger or embarrassment when her behavior was inappropriate or different from what was expected. At those times, we also felt angry at the world for judging and misunderstanding.

The behavior of children with these kinds of difficulties can also alienate friends and family. Although society's acceptance of disability has come a long way, a stigma still surrounds neurobiological illnesses such as childhood depression, bipolar disorder, obsessive-compulsive disorder, Tourette's syndrome, and others. Even if a child does not demonstrate outward behavior *problems*, their quirkiness, altered energy level, or mood may be looked upon in a negative way.

In recent years, the public has become more educated about some conditions, such as attention deficit disorder and autism spectrum disorders, but many challenges remain misunderstood. Much of society fears, misunderstands, and rejects those who behave in ways other than expected. This means parents and children who desperately need support and care do not receive it from the general public and, sadly, often not from churches and other faith-based organizations. Sometimes, parents wonder if they will survive the lonely road of special-needs parenting without losing their physical or mental health in the process.

As I write, I am reminded of the TV show *Wipeout*. In this game, each contestant has to overcome different obstacles to move on to the next stage. The obstacles include jumping through hoops, balancing on shaky or bumpy staircases, avoiding punching bags, and walking on slippery slopes. Almost every contestant loses his or her footing at least once per show and falls into the sometimes-muddy water below, yet most continue to enthusiastically face the next challenge.

As parents of kids with social, emotional, or behavioral struggles, we are also faced with a series of daunting challenges. Like the contestants on *Wipeout*, our first step is to realize we are up against a significant obstacle. Our next step is to try to move through the course, solving the medical or psychological puzzle of our child's illness and navigating the school system and social scene for the benefit of our child. While we do this, events inevitably alter the functioning of our family system—often putting marriages and sibling relationships at risk—so we have to work through those obstacles as well. And because of the genetic nature of many brain disorders, we might be hit with an additional challenge when we discover that a second child is also affected by neuropsychological difficulties.

As if this weren't difficult enough, an additional layer of complexity is added to the obstacle course as we *simultaneously* attempt to cope with our own worrisome thoughts, emotions, and questions. We wonder why God would allow this to happen and how we are going to deal with it. We may feel we don't have time to deal with our own emotional responses to the situation and try to push our sadness, fear, guilt, and anger aside so we can be "on" for the daily challenges. And then, when our child is unhappy or treated poorly, we experience a depth of emotional pain we never knew was possible. These complex emotions and questions can be crippling at times, and our feelings of aloneness can be overwhelming.

All of these obstacles are sizable and can send us reeling into muddy waters. However, getting back up, wiping off the muck, and re-entering the race are critically important. To this end, I have designed this book to intervene during these lonely times to help you feel understood and comforted when you most need it. My hope is to help you identify and overcome the spiritual, emotional, and thought obstacles that are likely to slip you up so you can move on and bless your children in the way God intends.

In this book, you will find insights from other parents in similar situations who have gone before you. All of the stories presented come from real-life families, although many of the names have been changed to ensure privacy. These stories will highlight common problems you will likely face as caregivers. In response to these problems, I will point to biblical answers to tough questions, and offer key spiritual, emotional, and cognitive principles to help heal the wounds and move you forward.

It is my intention that as you read this book you will see that help is available and feeling "wiped out" is not inevitable or permanent. I pray that you will meet your greatest source of hope and strength when you are wounded and weary: Jesus, the great physician, the one who loved (and loves) lepers, the chronically ill, sinners, and outcasts. I want you to be strengthened to continue on when life seems overwhelming so that you may someday share your own story of how God restored you and your children to the abundant living for which you were created.

So, parents, carry on now—and remember to tell your stories.

Chapter 1

GOT HOPE?

Don't you have any hope?" my mother asked me in a frantic voice. At that point in my life, I honestly did not. As a young mother, I had been devastated to discover that something was not well with Katie, my two-year-old daughter. This little girl was the apple of my eye. I had smothered her in kisses from the first day of her life, and I was sure she was the most beautiful baby in the world. How could something be wrong with her? How could this happen to me? How could I fix it? How could I live *without* fixing it? I was heartbroken and fearful of the future.

The cause of my emotional distress was Katie's troubling behavior. My once happy toddler with the blonde curls and blue eyes had begun to cringe in anxiety and run away from the kind people who tried to engage her. Playgroups had become stressful. Although Katie and I desperately needed social interaction, she would find subtle ways to avoid playing with other toddlers, leaving me with the task of facilitating play among the kids while the other mothers chatted. At home, she threw tantrums daily. Even driving had become stressful—she screamed any time I turned off the music when we arrived at our destination. I seemed unable to do much to soothe or placate her for long. This left me feeling frustrated, worried, and exhausted.

My husband, Bryan, and I were not sure what was wrong, and we struggled for more than a year to find the cause of Katie's anxiety and other behaviors. On some days Katie seemed okay but on other days she did not. As much as I wanted to believe the opinion of some professionals that it was just a temporary problem, deep down I knew it was more serious. Eighteen months and a few misdiagnoses later, Katie was finally diagnosed with autism at the age of three and a half.

Going through this process turned our nearly perfect world upside down. Bryan worked all day, which gave him some relief from the upheaval at home. I, in contrast, stopped work on my doctoral degree to focus on helping Katie. This meant my days and nights were filled with childcare duties and concern for her idiosyncrasies. Even lying in bed, my mind would wander to all the scary possibilities for the future. I wondered if she would make friends, if she would be ready for school in a few years, and if people would understand her and treat her well. During these sleepless nights, I would get up, pore over books about autism treatment, cry, and then read some more.

I soon became exhausted and overwhelmed. Not only did I have a difficult toddler, but I was also mother to our second daughter, Madeline, who was a colicky baby at the time. Being a natural introvert who thrived on quiet time and intellectual pursuits, I was nearly overwhelmed by the task of caring for and enriching the lives of two difficult children under the age of four. I struggled to read one more book, push one more swing, diffuse one more tantrum, and ease my infant through one more crying spell. I was chronically fatigued and depressed, yet I tried to put on a happy face for the sake of my two little girls.

My mother's question to me on that day made me realize just how hopeless I really was. How was I supposed to have hope? What was hope, anyway? Some sort of wishful thinking that everything will be okay? A handy form of delusion when faced with brutal reality? I was a realist by nature, and the reality of my daughter's situation seemed dismal to me. My concern over her struggles had squelched my joy, and in its place was a desperate and dogged determination to help Katie and survive my own fog of despair.

From Heartache to Hope

My story is not unique. In fact, research has shown that mothers of children with special needs are significantly more likely to become depressed than those with typical children.[1] We feel alone and overwhelmed, and the depth of these feelings can surprise us.

One of the initial causes for sadness is the realization that we have lost the child we had expected. Our dreams of enjoying our child's accomplishments and of sharing his or her development with family and friends suddenly become invaded by fear, doubt, and insecurity. Often we do not know which hopes are realistic for our child, and we might even be afraid to hope for much because the pain of our disappointment is almost unbearable. As a result, it is easy for sadness and hopelessness to infiltrate our families.

How is it, then, that some parents manage to look happy and hopeful in spite of their child having a disability? I remember marveling at these people early in my parenting journey. I wondered how could they look so carefree when it was obvious their child required a lot of intervention. I knew some of these people were born optimists and that hope came naturally to them as a personality trait. They had an innately positive outlook on life, worried about little, and expected the best in the face of difficulty.

But what about others like me, for whom worry is our middle name? I had anxiety built into the very fiber of my being, and to me, blind hope was the most unnatural outlook in the world. I did not expect positive outcomes unless there was a tangible reason to suspect them and I saw evidence of improvement. Even then, I was cautious about claiming success, because the potential consequences of letting down my guard were frightening. Was I doomed to constant anxiety? I didn't know how to come to the place where I would be able to hope in spite of the difficult reality.

1. What similar stories can you share about struggling with your child's early symptoms or the diagnosis you received?

    _____

    _____

    _____

2. What are your worries and heartache in the situation you are facing?

    _____

    _____

    _____

Hope and Faith Defined

In spite of my natural tendency to be a worrier, over time God taught me how to be a hopeful person regardless of the situation. This is no small miracle, as those who know me well can attest, and I am convinced that this development of hope in my life is evidence of God's power at work. Furthermore, because of this transformation God accomplished in me, I know that regardless of your personality or situation, God's power is available to give you hope and encouragement every day.

I had been a Christian for several years by the time of Katie's diagnosis, so I was pretty flabbergasted by my lack of hope. I wondered why I struggled so much with worry and pessimism and how I would ever gain a different outlook on life. For me, the question was twofold: (1) What actually is hope?, and (2) How do I get it? These questions motivated me to do some research and I want to share with you several concepts I found during my study. Let me warn you—there is a lot of information in the first part of this chapter so you will not want to read it in a hurry. Please take time to let it sink in and be in prayer for the Holy Spirit to guide your heart and mind.

Webster's Dictionary defines hope as "to desire with expectation of fulfillment; to expect with confidence."[2] This is not the same thing as a *wish,* which, according to the dictionary, is something we "have a desire for" but do not necessarily expect to see fulfilled. There is an important distinction between the two, for with hope there is an *expectation* of gratification.

We also need to explore how the Bible describes hope. In Psalm 33:18, we read, "But the eyes of the LORD are on those who fear him, on those whose *hope is in his unfailing love*" (emphasis added). The biblical hope in this passage contains an expectation of fulfillment because it is focused on God's unfailing love. This means that our hope depends on our belief in God and in His love. Clearly, what or in whom we hope is key to our expectation of fulfillment. This verse also reveals that God watches out for those who place their hopes in His love. Let's take a few moments to explore this assertion in the life of a worried parent who lived many years before us.

3. Read Genesis 16. When Hagar flees into the wilderness due to Sarai's mistreatment, who visits her there?

    _____

    _____

    _____

4. How does Hagar describe the one who comforts and directs her?

    _____

    _____

    _____

5. In Hebrew, one of the names for God is *El Roi,* which means "the strong one who sees me." These are the characteristics of God that Hagar identified in Genesis 16:13. Do you believe He is strong and that He sees you? (It's okay to be honest).

    _____

    _____

    _____

6. If so, what does it mean to you personally to know that God sees you in your distress?

_____

_____

_____

If you believe in God's unfailing love, write Psalm 33:18 on an index card. Find a place to put this card in your home and/or workplace so you are reminded to reflect upon the fact that God sees you and will direct you in your distress.

7. If you are unsure of God's unfailing love, write your reasons here and please read on.

_____

_____

_____

This first part of our discussion of hope rests on our belief and expectation that God loves us without fail and that He sees us and responds to our afflictions.

Next, let's look at Hebrews 11:1, as it gives us a bit more insight into hope by bringing faith into the equation. It reads, "Faith is the substance of things hoped for, the evidence of things not seen" (KJV). In other words, the meat of what we hope for is dependent on faith as the substance to back it up—there can be no real hope without it. In the same way that gold held by the US Treasury was originally used to validate the American dollar, so faith is necessary to back up our hope. Not only that, but *faith is the currency, the substance, and the power* to receive what we hope for. Without faith, hope is just wishful thinking, empty of power and meaning.

This raises the question of how we can muster up faith so we can have hope. How do we work on getting the faith we need so badly? It sounds like an elusive task if you ask me—I mean, how does one just "get faith"? Thankfully, the Bible tells us it is not up to us to *get* faith, but to just *accept* it as a gift from God (see Ephesians 2:8; Philippians 1:29). Similarly, Hebrews 12:2 tells us that Jesus is the "author and perfecter of

Faith is the currency, the substance, and the power to receive what we hope for.

our faith." Jesus designs it and gives it to us, and we must just accept His gift. So, we are in partnership with God on this faith issue—He does His part (the giving), and we do our part (the receiving).

This sounds almost too easy to be true, doesn't it? Often we do not think of faith as something we *receive* but as something that is *built* based on testing and experience. We have faith that our car will get us to a desired destination because it does so most of the time. We have faith that our work will earn us a paycheck and that our paycheck will secure us food and shelter. Each day, we put our faith in something, test it, and based on *our view* of the outcome, our faith will either be built or diminished. Many people treat their faith in God the same way, and He can live up to that test. However, the crux of this matter really rests in "our view of the outcome." Each day our faith has the opportunity to grow, but this somewhat depends on our ability to increasingly see things as God might see them. We do not have God's all encompassing view here on earth, so we need to ask Him how to interpret the different events that happen in our lives. For now, we will leave that concept and touch on it again later.

8. How are wishes different from hope?

_____

_____

_____

9. What is the relationship between faith and hope?

_____

_____

_____

10. How do we get faith? What might affect how it grows?

_____

_____

_____

_____

Bear with me now. I know this is a long discussion, but by the end you will have a better understanding of just what hope is and how important it is to your life. Believe me, without it, your chances of keeping the joy and strength needed to raise your child are greatly diminished. You will need every ounce of hope you can get.

As a review, we have discovered that the gift of faith is a key component in our ability to develop hope. However, The Bible tells us there are other ways to develop hope, as well. Evidence is found in Romans 5:2-5, where Paul writes, "We rejoice in the hope of the glory of God. Not only so, but we also rejoice in our sufferings, because we know that suffering produces perseverance; perseverance, character; and character, hope. And hope does not disappoint us, because God has poured out his love into our hearts by the Holy Spirit, whom he has given us."

Based on this verse, it appears that our role as we walk through life—including times of suffering—is to accept and use *any* gift of faith God gives to us to *persevere*. As we use God's gifts and persevere, our character is improved in a godly way. This, in turn, leads to hope when we find that God has proven Himself faithful by providing love and care during our suffering. Because God has poured His love into our hearts by the gift of the Holy Spirit (see Romans 5:5), we are able to interpret this love and care as coming from God, and not as just a coincidence.

Again, our ability and willingness to interpret provisions as coming from God is key to our faith and to our hope. Sometimes the provisions come almost effortlessly when something or someone offers help without our toil. At other times the help comes only through suffering, perseverance, and the building of character. But the provisions still come from God—that is the bottom line. The Holy Spirit allows us to see this truth.

11. Write Romans 5:2-5 in the space below. What is a benefit of persevering through times of suffering?

_____

_____

_____

_____

_____

_____

_____

12. Think about a time of suffering that you endured (or are enduring) in your life. How did that suffering lead to perseverance?

_____

_____

_____

13. Did your suffering and perseverance lead to developing godly character? How?

_____

_____

_____

14. Where would you identify yourself today on the hope continuum?

_____

_____

_____

Hope and Faith Gained

Given the Bible's explanation about how hope is gained, it has become more clear to me why I lacked hope regarding the future of my special-needs child. In my childhood and early adulthood, I rarely had to engage in much struggling or suffering to fulfill my desires, and as a result, I was not faced with situations that would have tested and built on my initially smaller gift of faith. It seemed I was able to overcome every challenge I encountered based on my own skill and effort. I realize now how arrogant my thinking was, as certainly many blessings materialized due to the prayers of my parents and God's love and goodness. Nonetheless, my daughter's autism was the first problem in my life I _felt_ unable to fix. It was my first experience with something I could identify as bigger than me. Although I could help Katie, no effort or skill on my part could make the autism go away completely.

This problem provided a perfect opportunity for God to show me His power and build my faith. The hard part was developing my mustard-seed-sized faith into a greater faith and hope. My hope had to grow just as Paul predicted in Romans 5:3—through suffering, perseverance, and the hard-won development of godly character. There were no shortcuts. It was a painful but necessary way for God to convince me of His unfailing love. The process was effective, however, and now I can truly "rejoice in the hope of the glory of God" (Romans 5:2), regardless of the circumstances.

God's Provisions

Being the cautious person I am, my hope did not appear overnight but developed little by little over months and years of experience. It grew as I began to see God's divine care and love for Katie and me in practical ways. As I look back now on that time in my life, I am amazed at all the things God provided for our family to help us survive and even occasionally thrive.

One of God's provisions was the comfort and rest He gave me. He had already given me my husband, Bryan, who was willing to sit in the two-year-old Sunday school class for three months until our little girl felt safe enough to go there alone. What a blessing this was! During this time, I was able to attend a women's Bible class led by Teresa, a woman who exemplified God's victory in her life in spite of her lifelong struggle with mental illness. God knew how hopeless and frightened I was, and He wisely sent me to this woman to show me that *disability and illness do not have to overcome His people!* It was just what I needed. In addition, God opened the doors for a small preschool to admit Katie, even though she was not yet potty trained. This gave me much-needed respite.

Later, as Katie grew, God provided teachers who appreciated her many gifts as well as her quirks. They highlighted her fabulous memory and excellent reading ability. Although Katie struggled with anxiety and mastering social skills, God blessed us with a principal whose creative thinking helped her remain in a Christian school until sixth grade. In middle school, God provided a charter homeschool program that met Katie's changing needs. He also put into place a soccer coach who worked to help her be successful in the sport she loved.

Katie would tell you that the annual Bible camp she attended was a place where God encouraged her in significant ways. She was also thankful for the small group of girls from her soccer team who remained her faithful friends even when they attended different schools. During high school, God allowed some excellent (though painful) learning experiences to take place in her life, which further helped her to grow. He placed a few kind peers at her school and a church family to support her on her path. As I watched God work in her life and saw all the ways He provided to meet our physical and emotional needs, my faith slowly grew. This faith has now become the substance of my hope for an unknown future.

I know many parents of special-needs children who have also experienced God's intervention in their lives. One such person is my friend Erin, who has a seven-year-old boy with Tourette's syndrome, ADHD, and possibly other mental illnesses. She told me one day, "We absolutely cannot get our son to stop running on the furniture, yelling, snorting, spitting, licking, hitting, kissing, growling, biting … the list goes on and on. Most days we are just barely hanging in there. But then God blesses us with a beautiful day or two when we desperately need it … and we always know that it could be a lot worse than it is."

Erin acknowledges that a "beautiful day or two" at just the right time is a gift from God. It is God's love, revealed in the form of such provisions, that keeps her faith and hope alive. I believe God's gift of the Holy Spirit has allowed both of us to interpret even His smallest provisions as love letters to us, which in turn has enabled us to recognize they are from God and not just a result of chance or coincidence. It is as if His love gets sewn into our hearts, sealing the hope that He will walk us through the next problem. Our question then changes from *whether* God will help us to *how and when* He will help us. What a beautiful new assurance!

15. What glimpses of hope have you seen (or are you seeing) through your experience of suffering?

_____

_____

_____

Continuing Challenges and a Relationship with God

It is important to keep in mind that God's provisions did not and will not alleviate every painful experience we encounter. In my and Erin's situation, our families did not receive immediate reassurance that our children's futures would be successful. As we look back on Katie's childhood, my family remembers the painful experiences as clearly as the provisions. Later on, we watched our second child develop chronic health problems complicated by depression and anxiety. This threw our family into crisis a second time, though we were stronger by then and are recovering more quickly.

As you wrestle with your personal challenges, I want you to remember that God provided for the needs in our family, but the provisions usually came against a background of struggle. Like the manna God sent His people in the wilderness (see Exodus 16), He provided help to us after we were close to giving up and cried out for Him to intercede. As we have walked through our own wilderness experience over the years, we have seen a pattern of God providing just enough for our children to get us through the trial, and yet this has been enough to grow our faith and hope.

I must admit I sometimes wish God would take His magic wand, solve all our problems in one fell swoop, and put a sign on our lives that says, "And they lived happily every after."

Although the childish part of me wants this type of fairy-godmother approach, God's decision to send only a daily supply of provisions has actually been a bigger blessing in our lives. Why? Because it has kept us continually dependent and prodded us into constant contact and fellowship with Him. If He were to hand us a lifetime of support without us having to ask, we would be inclined to forget Him as the giver and take the gifts for granted. He knows it is in our best interest to give us just what we need so that our relationship and dependence on Him will continue to develop. He knows we will not benefit as much from tangible blessings without that relationship.

I believe one of the reasons God gives us children is so we can better understand His love for us. Just as we want a relationship with our children so they will listen to our advice and lead a better life, God wants us to talk and listen to Him and heed His good counsel. The great mystery of God's provision is that the best gift He can give us is simply Himself. His greatest promise to us is that He will never leave us or forsake us (see Hebrews 13:5). Sometimes, He has to catch our attention in dramatic ways so we will recognize and accept this great gift.

> The great mystery of God's provision is that the best gift He can give us is simply Himself.

16. Review Hebrews 13:5. How has God's presence been a gift to you?

_____

_____

_____

Today, God continues to provide for my children as they transition into adulthood and independent living. Am I frightened sometimes? Yes. Do I often fail to see how we will overcome the next challenge? You bet. Do I have hope that God will provide? Most definitely. I recently read a wonderful definition of hope by an unknown author: "Hope is fixing our desires on the promises of God, and not doubting in the darkness what He has shown us in the light." This reminds me that when I fear the future, I can rest in the reality of His past faithfulness.

I love how David expresses his assurance of God's care in Psalm 5:1-3. Even in a dark time, David was able to say, "Give ear to my words, O Lord, consider my sighing. Listen to my cry for help, my King and my God, for to you I pray. In the morning, O Lord, you hear my voice; in the morning *I lay my requests before you and wait in expectation*" (emphasis added). Note that David says he waits in expectation! He was completely confident that God would hear, listen to, and answer his prayers. Like David, we can also experience great assurance that God will come through in our time of need.

Capturing Hope

Years have passed since my mother asked me if I had any hope and my heart responded by wondering what hope actually was. Through many trials, I have learned that hope is not just wishful thinking but the assurance of God's love and care made known to us through the work of the Holy Spirit. *Hope is built on a faith that tells us God loves our children even more than we do—and that we can trust Him.*

Today, when I experience difficulty and concern over my children, I try to remember that these times represent opportunities to build my faith in God's love. Proverbs 15:13 tells us "heartache crushes the spirit," but Psalm 146:5 says, "Blessed is he ... whose hope is in the LORD his God." What I want to impress on you is that *the first and most important battle you must win as a special-needs parent is to capture hope in God.* You must win the battle over despair concerning your current circumstances, and expect that God will provide at the right time.

Maybe you are like I was as a young parent, and do not have a long track record of crediting God for the successes in your life. If so, God's Word is available for you to witness His provisions in the lives of others (you might start by reading Hebrews chapters 11 and 12). You *can* receive the gift of faith that God offers you and capture the hope He has set before you. Winning this battle will take a childlike surrender of your controlling nature, but it is worth waving that white flag. Capturing hope will set the stage for everything else that takes place in your life.

Proverbs 4:23 states, "Above all else, guard your heart, for it is the wellspring of life." If you have not already done so, get in the habit of protecting your heart by asking God for faith. Then look for His provisions each day, no matter how small they may seem. (Remember that even seemingly small provisions can add up to be meaningful in the long run.) As you do this, you will see that God will not disappoint you, and as a result, your faith will be built up and your hope will set in.

Remembering His Provisions

A helpful task to begin the hope-building process is to keep an "Evidence of Hope Record." To get into the habit of seeing God's intervention in your life, I encourage you to do this for at least the next ten weeks. Be faithful to write down at least one instance every two weeks of how God provided something to help you get through a challenging situation. You can write this evidence in a journal, or use the spaces provided below. If you are in a Persevering Parent support group, remember to occasionally share these provisions with others in your group.

Keep in mind that if you are going through a difficult period, it may take ten months—or even ten *years*—to see a significant change. Change can be slow, but the small steps you take each day will lead the way. If you are faithful to keep this record, someday when you are feeling hopeless you will be able to look back and see all the times that God has provided.

Evidence of Hope Record

Weeks 1-2

_____

_____

_____

_____

_____

Weeks 3-4

_____

_____

_____

_____

Weeks 5-6

_____

_____

_____

_____

Weeks 7-8

_____

_____

_____

_____

_____

Weeks 9-10

_____

_____

_____

_____

As you can see, it is critical to develop a heart filled with trust in God. If you feel you do not have the gift of faith that allows you to do this, now is a good time to ask for it. Below is a simple prayer you can pray to help you with this task.

Prayer Thought

Lord, please give me faith that You love me, my family, and my child, and help me to accept this gift. Help me know that no matter how difficult life gets, You are here beside me, ready to give comfort and provide for our needs. Help me to persevere through suffering and develop godly character so my hope in You becomes deep. Thank You, Lord, for answering this prayer. Amen.

Chapter 2

LIVING YOUR NEW NORMAL

I recently visited an old friend who has a twelve-year-old daughter. This girl is one of those kids who seemed to have no need for a parent after she could walk, talk, use the bathroom, and feed herself. I believe that had the need arisen, she could have raised herself once she received her kindergarten diploma. She determines how much time she needs to get ready in the morning and reach her destination, and then she sets her own alarm and *actually gets up*. She makes As and Bs in school, is engaged in after-school activities, and is active in her church youth group. She is a good citizen, a friend to others, and a helper around the house. This is expected and typical behavior for the 12-year-old in this family. It is their "normal."

However, "normal" in our family—and in the families of many neurologically challenged kids—looks a lot different. For example, I recently came across a picture of one of my children at a birthday party at around age nine or ten. It was definitely not one of her best birthday pictures, and it was certainly not one I would send to relatives at Christmastime, but it is memorable to me. The birthday party was at Chuck E. Cheese—a glorious place for most children—but in this picture, my child has a sour look on her face and is stomping across the floor, angry and glaring.

I do not remember what angered her at that moment, and I'm not sure what prompted me to take this picture. However, I think it was a tiny voice in my head telling me to record life as it really was as opposed to what I would have liked it to be. Even though the situation was not pleasant, a small part of me had to giggle at her antics. In some small way, I wanted a memory of my child in print as I had seen her so often in person during that time of her life. For a variety of reasons, angry was our daughter's "normal" for a while, and it affected the entire family.

Accepting the New Normal

Accepting the new normal that comes with a child who is challenged with a disability, illness, or special need is always difficult because our culture is obsessed with what it considers normal. Both of my children with special needs have at one time said to me, "I just want to be normal," and as a parent, my first thought for them was the same. Of course I wanted my children to fit in, feel accepted, and not struggle any more than other kids. My first goal was for them to be as normal as possible. I worked to make it happen, and believed our family would be happy if we attained it. However, the reality is that even though our children have made great progress, we have had to accept that the special needs differentiate us from other families we know.

> More than 20 percent of children in the United States have had a *seriously debilitating* mental disorder at some point in their young lives.

While on the topic of acceptance, I want to clarify that I am not talking about accepting *every one* of our children's behaviors. Certainly, there are some behaviors we cannot condone or accept for the long term, even if we need to tolerate them for a time. For instance, harming themselves or others is not an ongoing behavior we can accept in our kids, even if they have neurological challenges. We must do our best to get these behaviors under control. This is a topic for another discussion, however. For the purposes of this chapter, I am talking about the struggle to accept that our kids, for better or worse, are different than other kids, and that they are likely to stay different in some ways for their lifetime.

Unfortunately, being seen as different in our society often equates to being perceived as difficult or weird. Although we may not want to admit it, knowing that others might see our child this way is hurtful and embarrassing. The differences can cause us to feel that we are alone in our struggles and that nobody understands or accepts our child. This feeling of isolation is certainly one of the most difficult problems facing families with challenged children. In fact, perhaps one of the reasons why you picked up this book (or someone bought it for you) is because you need comforting words to confirm that you are not alone and that someone understands your life.

No matter how alone we might feel, the truth is that many families experience similar struggles and *do* understand what you are going through. In fact, the Center for Disease Control estimates that 20 percent of families in the United States are affected by a disability.[3] Furthermore, a 2010 report from the National Institute of Mental Health reveals that more than 20 percent of children in the United States have had a seriously debilitating mental disorder at some point in their lives.[4] This number does not even include neurological disorders such as autism, Tourette's syndrome, traumatic brain injuries, seizures, and others.

One reason why parents *feel* like they are among a small population of others dealing with a disabled or difficult child is that the 80 percent of the population without special needs doesn't pay much attention to the minority of the population—*until* they find themselves part of it. Clearly this all changes when you become the parent of a child with a special need. Again, the statistics reveal that a significant subset of parents in the United States *are* dealing with social, emotional, or behavioral symptoms in their children similar to what you are experiencing in your home. You might just not have met these people yet.

Normality Redefined

I can certainly relate to the strangeness of having to deal with this new normal of social, emotional, or behavioral turmoil. I grew up in a relatively sheltered and calm environment, and I could never have imagined some of the difficulties my current family has had to endure. Having to hold my young daughter to the floor to contain her rage was certainly one of the things I could never have imagined doing. It would have been too strange and horrible for me even to consider. However, after exhausting other options, my husband and I were trained to use this behavior technique. When we applied it and Katie was screaming the worst words she knew at us, I remember thinking, *How can this be happening to us?* The good news is that while this particular experience was unhappy, it lasted for just a season in our lives.

Years later, after we had gone through a number of difficulties, I learned that other families of children with disabilities had experiences similar to those in our household. Although it was not typical in the family in which I was raised, it was quite normal in this population of special-needs families. I was not unique or alone as a parent of a special-needs child—and neither are you. The following are some of the experiences of real-life families who have struggled with a illness or disability in the family.

In families with children affected by autism, anxiety, attention deficit disorder, mood disorders, or other neurobiological problems, "normal" life looks much different from the general population. For example, I know a mom whose depressed child often states she would rather die than go to school when she wakes in the morning. In this family, the mom has to balance the importance of a good education for her child against just helping her child face the basic demands of life. Another mom, whose child has bipolar disorder, might find herself looking around the neighborhood for her son who ran away after she asked him to get ready for a family celebration. This family might have to deal with the chaos of finding their child and also respond to disapproving relatives who do not understand why standard punishment for such behavior is not effective.

In families with children who have anger or behavior outbursts, parents may have to take turns "standing guard" in front of one child's bedroom to protect him or her from an aggressive sibling. A dad's normal might be to physically pull his child with oppositional defiant disorder out of the neighborhood softball game because his child cannot be a "good loser" when his team is behind. It may seem normal for parents to have to repair a hole in their child's bedroom because their child kicked or punched the wall. There are children who cannot bond well and push parental affection away, as occurs in children with reactive attachment disorder.

Children with sensory or anxiety difficulties also shape what is considered normal in their homes. The police might be called because a neighbor was concerned that child abuse was taking place, only to discover the child has screamed for thirty minutes because his potatoes were touching his beans on the plate. It is common for families of preschoolers with autism to turn a dining room into a therapy room to accommodate hours of sensory and/or behavioral intervention. Parents of a child with obsessive-compulsive disorder may have to accommodate elaborate rituals every night just so their child can fall asleep.

Other families of children with disabilities not considered social, emotional, or behavioral in nature also share many of these same feelings. For a family with a deaf child, for instance, normal might be practicing reading lips at the dinner table. Because yelling to a deaf child is ineffective, parents may have the exhausting task of running after their child several times a day to warn him or her about potential danger, or just to get the child's attention so they can communicate with sign language.

For families who have children with physical or developmental handicaps, normal might mean tube feeding at the dinner table or hand feeding by a family member. It might mean cleaning ostomy or insulin pump sites, making regular hospital visits, bathing, and changing sanitary napkins or diapers of older children. Many parents' new normal might also include homeschooling, giving up date nights, skipping extended family outings, micromanaging their child's daily routine, frequent trips to doctors and therapists, excessive work and worry at the beginning of each new school year, and continuous education of teachers, neighbors, family, and friends about their child's special needs.

1. What are some of the circumstances that make up your new normal day? What events tire, frustrate, or overwhelm you?

   _____

   _____

   _____

2. In spite of the challenges, what new normal circumstances teach you or make you smile?

_____

_____

_____

3. What situation in your new normal life is difficult for you to accept?

_____

_____

_____

4. What could you do to accept or partially accommodate this situation?

_____

_____

_____

5. If you were to "let go" of this situation, what is the worst that could happen?

_____

_____

_____

Normality Overrated

For parents with children who develop any of these difficulties, these new normals are frightening and almost unbelievable. At first, the situation can seem unreal—much like a bad dream. However, like other parents, you will learn to cope and survive. The unusual things you must do to make your family work will become a routine part of life. You will learn that you are more flexible than you thought, and you will gain skills and insights that can even help you thrive in your circumstances.

As I mentioned, one of the biggest hindrances to families accepting their new normal is society's attitude about normality. Given this, it is important to remember that normal kids can also be a source of stress for their parents. *Merriam-Webster's Dictionary* defines normal as "conforming to a type, standard or regular" condition. It does not necessarily describe a condition that is always desirable or even best.[5] For example, it is normal for 40–50 percent of families in America today to be broken by divorce.[6] It is typical for American teenage girls to become obsessed with their weight and physical appearance, and for college-age boys to routinely engage in binge drinking. These "normal" behaviors are not so appealing. Could it be that normal is a bit overrated?

> Could it be that "normal" is a bit overrated?

To add some perspective to the relative importance of normality, let's consider the lives of some biblical heroes and compare them to the norm of their day. It's clear that many of God's chosen people encountered a difficult or abnormal situation along their paths to heroism. Joseph was sold into slavery and later spent time in an Egyptian prison, which was *not* the standard way people achieved the position of authority he later attained. Jacob, a deceiver, was left with an *abnormal* gait—a limp—after a struggle with God's angel, yet God allowed him to be part of a miraculous plan. Rahab, a prostitute, became an example of faith because she welcomed Israel's spies into the Promised Land. It is surprising—and *not normal*—that a prostitute would be included in the "Hall of Fame" in Hebrews 11.

Moses, a Hebrew baby boy, was placed in the Nile River by his mother and then plucked out and raised by Pharaoh's daughter, which was *not* the regular way children were raised. It was certainly *not normal* behavior for Moses, as a young Egyptian prince, to kill an Egyptian guard and escape into the desert for forty years. From the world's perspective, Moses' fall from his noble upbringing can only be seen as evidence of big-time failure.

New Testament heroes also lived through less-than-ideal situations. Mary, the mother of Jesus, was pregnant out of wedlock, which was certainly *not* a healthy situation for her. Jesus was born in a stable with no midwife or other female family help, which was *not the regular* practice. And the apostle Paul was stricken with an *undesirable* "thorn" that God allowed him to have, even though Paul asked for it to be taken away.

It is clear that some of God's chosen people had what we would consider abnormal and often negative circumstances in their lives. God seems to have no hang-ups with what we would consider normal. So why should we?

Set Apart

It should not surprise us that many of God's chosen people did not fit into the "normal box," because He has always had unique plans for His people. He never planned for them to blend in with society. Rather, He intended His people to be set apart for His own purposes (see Exodus 19:6). He commanded the Hebrew nation to be circumcised, follow an abnormal diet, and refrain from intermarriage with other peoples (see Genesis 17:10; Leviticus 11; Deuteronomy 7:1–3). Unlike the "normal" people around them, who worshiped many gods, the Hebrews were to accept and worship the one and only God (see Exodus 20:3). In return, God promised His protection, provision, care, and discipline. He promised the Hebrew nation that they would be blessed and would be a blessing to the world (see Genesis 12:2-3).

The same God asks us today not to "conform to the pattern of this world"—or to be normal by the standards of this world—but to be "transformed" in our hearts and minds (Romans 12:2). God invites us to conform to the pattern of heaven—the world that is truly our home. So, while we want our children and families to blend in with society, it is really *not* essential that we fit into the culture around us. Moses described himself as an alien and foreigner in the desert where God primed him for his life's work (see Exodus 2:22). Likewise, the author of Hebrews tells us how Abraham was faithful to God because he longed for his heavenly home (see Hebrews 11:8-10). I wonder how much he would have longed for God's goodness if he had felt comfortable and at home during all his time on earth.

Similarly, dealing with disabilities and/or challenges provides us with a powerful impetus to accept God's invitation to be part of His heavenly world. This is a world that values things opposite to what our physical world values. It is a world in which "God chose the weak things of the world to shame the strong" (1 Corinthians 1:27). It is a world in which "many who are first will be last, and many who are last will be first" (Matthew 19:30). It is a place in which God infuses power into our weakness that is beyond our understanding and ability to replicate in other ways.

> God infuses power into our weakness that is beyond our understanding and ability to replicate.

One of my favorite books is *The Power of the Powerless* by Christopher de Vinck. In this book, the author describes how his family cared for his severely disabled brother, Oliver, who was unable to talk, move, or feed himself. For over thirty years, until Oliver's death, de Vinck family members took turns feeding Oliver, bathing him, and turning him over in his bed.[7] It was their "normal" to love him each day in this way. Of course, to most of the American world, this situation and the family's choice to keep Oliver in their home might be considered abnormal. (And what a beautifully abnormal family it was!)

In his book, de Vinck describes how Oliver, in his powerlessness, had a curious power of defining and clarifying love in those around him. His "powerless" condition proved to be a testing ground for those who met him, as the quality of a person's character became clear when he or she interacted with Oliver.

The kind of character to which God calls us is similar to the character demonstrated by the de Vinck family members. It is a kind of character that is gentle, compassionate, giving, and loving. It represents a mindset that is contrary to the normal thinking of the world, which tries to convince us that our time is better spent with someone or something that can give back to us. Oliver's mother could have chosen a career outside the home or become involved in activities like other moms were doing. It would have been easier for her to do so—as it would be for us not to have to deal with the struggles of special-needs parenting. However, it would have been a loss, for these struggles refined the de Vinck family, making them more compassionate, understanding, loving, and powerful. The same will be true in our situation if we allow God to do His refining work in our lives.

Getting Over It

If we claim to be set apart by God and a member of His family, why do we still struggle with the desire to be normal in the world's eyes? Of course, it is natural for us to respond this way in the natural world, but to put it bluntly, we need to get over it! I do not say this lightly, as I know from experience that it can take years to adjust to raising a special-needs child and that the process can be painful. However, once we understand that our goal is not to mimic the "normal" world, but to pattern our lives on Christ, it becomes easier for us to accept the uniqueness of our families and our lives.

> Once we understand that our goal is not to mimic the "normal" world, but to pattern our lives on Christ, it becomes easier for us to accept the uniqueness of our families and our lives.

A friend of mine once told me that her family's motto was, "Normal is just a setting on the washing machine." I like this analogy. Our child with special needs is different from what the world would describe as normal because he or she requires more care, like the "delicates" or "hand-washables" selection on a washing machine. Are these articles of clothing less valuable because they need special care? No. But they might *seem* less desirable in our fast-paced society, where people are too impatient to take time for special-care fabrics. In fact, textile designers and those who appreciate fabrics know that the most valuable and fine fabrics often take the most care to preserve. They are more expensive to produce and more expensive to maintain. Gentle detergents and hand-washing is needed to properly care for them. They involve much more work, but the outcome—the reward—is beautiful and noteworthy.

Our special-needs child might not be normal in the sense of usual or common, and he or she might require more work, time, and energy on our part. Sometimes, we may long for easy-care, wash-and-wear type kids—the cotton and polyester type of children. But God has entrusted us with His delicate, special-care person—one who is more like silk, satin, or linen. He or she is shiny and beautiful when well cared for, which glorifies the Maker in a unique way.

The challenge for us is to recognize the beauty of our child even in the absence of normality in our lives. As we will discuss in upcoming chapters, sometimes we cannot see the beauty for a season, but we need to remember it is there. Seeing the hidden beauty in people is a big part of what Jesus did during His ministry. He ministered to those on the fringe of society—those considered different or not good enough. As parents of children with special needs, we have the opportunity to do the same. We can spread God's love right where we are through our new normal experiences. As we do, we will begin to view differences the way Jesus viewed them: as a reason to reach out and love.

6. In what ways have you personally seen normality as overrated?

_____

_____

_____

7. As Christians, we are set apart for something greater than normality. Is there anything holding you back from the transformation to which God has called you? If so, what?

_____

_____

_____

From Evil to Good

Now, we have to be real about this. Sometimes it is difficult in our at-home ministries to see the deep beauty or character growth that can result from our child's difficulties. We feel sorry for ourselves and for our child—sorry that our child's unusual, disruptive, or isolating behavior creates pain for him or her and for us. We see the effort and tears that result from the illness or disability, but not the good. Sure, we may know that our hearts have become more compassionate or that our relationship with God has grown, but often, in our minds, these positives do not outweigh the negatives. We cannot see any *tangible* perks as a result of the disability, so we have a hard time accepting our new lives and the host of difficulties they bring.

In the book of Genesis, we read the story of a man named Joseph, who was also faced with a number of overwhelming difficulties—situations that would have caused anyone to wonder what possible good could come out of them. Joseph began his life as the favored child of his father, Jacob. He was a confident child, and one day he bragged to his brothers about his father's gift of a multicolored coat and his lofty dreams of the future. Joseph's brothers grew jealous of him, and soon Joseph, the "golden boy," became a young man who was brutally sold into slavery (see Genesis 37). Overnight, his life changed from normal to not only abnormal but also, by most standards, horrific.

Over the next several years, Joseph worked as a slave in a foreign land and served time in jail for a crime he did not commit (see Genesis 39). How fair is that? But while the temptation to fight against these injustices would have been understandable, Joseph chose to cope with his new normal life by gaining strength from his relationship with God and making the best of his situation. Instead of throwing a pity party with his cellmates and wondering what all the other shepherd boys back home were doing, he demonstrated character and wisdom, and eventually he was made caretaker of the jail while still a prisoner. After Joseph's release, God arranged for him to be promoted to a position second only to the pharaoh of Egypt (see Genesis 41:40). In this role, he developed a nationwide food storage program that later relieved a famine in the land (see Genesis 41:47-49).

Joseph's life proves that something tangible, good, and literally life-saving can come from a family tragedy. Are we so sure our lives are any different? Are we so sure no tangible good can come from the difficult situations in which we find ourselves? Do we think no one will find strength or encouragement from watching us faithfully wade through our trials? Of course others will gain strength from watching us! Much like Joseph, who chose to forgive his brothers who sold him into slavery (see Genesis 50:20), we can choose to forgive whomever or whatever we have been blaming for our problems. We can look for evidence that God intended the difficulties to accomplish good. We really can see our new lives as stepping stones on the path to God's goodness.

None of us likes to accept imperfection in our families. We do not like change that involves grief, uncertainty, or lots of work. We struggle against accepting it and want to cower in self-pity. We keep looking to more "normal" families and striving to be like them. Perhaps in an effort to force our children into a more normal landing pattern, we even valiantly don our super-parent capes. We fly about for a while, sometimes for years, solving problems right and left. However, while we must do our best to help our children, in the end, no spandex suit or cape can solve all the challenges of a special-needs child. We have to *accept* our new normal and, in the wee hours of the morning when sleep will not come, ask God to provide the spiritual, emotional, and physical recharging we so desperately need.

8. What is something that inspires or teaches you from the story of Joseph's life?

_____

_____

_____

How can you apply this to your situation?

_____

_____

Learning to Thrive in the New Normal

Once we accept our situation and turn to God for help, we have to develop some routines that will help us thrive in our new normal. While there is no magic formula that works in every situation, parents of socially, emotionally, or behaviorally challenged children agree that doing the following is a good start:

1. *Accept that your new life will not be the same as it was before, but that there will still be joy and good times.* In John 17:13, Jesus said He came that we might experience the full measure of His joy. When He spoke these words, He was not talking to a group of perfect people but to His disciples, all of whom were—and are—flawed, sinful, and different in some way.
2. *Walk through the challenges of each day one step at a time and don't look too far into the future.* In Matthew 6:34, Jesus tells us not to worry about tomorrow, for tomorrow will worry about itself. In other words, each day has enough trouble of its own. Isn't that the truth! Of course, this doesn't mean we shouldn't make plans for the future, but we should not *worry* about the future. We can do one without the other—though if worry has become a habit, we must make a conscious effort to stop ourselves once we start down that path. (We will explore this topic in more detail in Chapter 10).

3. *Join a support group.* Attend an educational or online support group, or just look for one or two other moms or families with whom you can talk when you're having a bad day. You will eventually find someone who will understand your situation and this will help immensely.

4. *Hire a behavior coach.* Seek professional help if your child becomes stuck in an inappropriate behavior—especially if others in the family start reacting inappropriately to it. Sometimes the entire family can get caught in a negative behavior cycle that begins with one child, and it can take outside eyes to see the problem and break the chain.

5. *Get counseling for yourself (or other family members) when you feel particularly discouraged, weary, depressed, or anxious.* This is critical because behaviors in a family can feed on each other, especially if you are the mom. As the old saying goes, "If mama ain't happy, ain't nobody happy." Good counseling can do wonders. You may even wish you had gone sooner.

6. *Regularly secure respite care or babysitting to give you a break.* It is amazing how much better you will like your children if you *regularly* get the chance to spend a little bit of time away from them.

7. *Take time to nurture other important relationships.* Set aside time for your spouse or significant other, even if it is hard to find time or childcare. The investment you make will be worth the hassle.

8. *Pray unceasingly, and expect God to answer your prayers for wisdom in raising your child (see James 1:5-6).* You will feel more confident in making tricky parenting decisions when you know you've sought God's advice first.

9. *Be educated.* Learn all you can about the particular problem or disability you and your family are dealing with so you will be educated on what might be happening within your child.

10. *Keep up a hobby.* Engage in a hobby or activity you enjoy so you can still tap into the person you were before you became a special-needs parent.

11. *Take steps to reduce the stress.* Reduce stress with exercise, warm baths, gardening, or other healthy activities that soothe you.

12. *Dig into God's Word with fervor.* If you need discipline and guidance in this area, consider joining a Bible study. Many people can testify that it was during times of trial that God's Word came alive for them. Often, the first time we really "see" or understand God is when we turn to Him during a crisis. This was true of Job in the Bible, who, after enduring the death of his children, the destruction of his business, and painful health problems, spoke these words to God: "My ears had heard of you but now my eyes have seen you" (Job 42:5).

Again, while none of these activities will solve every problem, they will improve your ability to manage difficulties. They are simple suggestions, but are powerful if you practice them. As they become healthy new normal activities over time, you will find new ways to cope with the challenges and will gain insight and understanding that will help you in the future. Be assured that the process *does* become easier over time.

9. Which of these practical activities and actions do you need to implement in your life to help you thrive?

_____

_____

_____

What others you would add?

_____

Working with Your New Normal

As I look back, perhaps taking that picture I earlier described of my child at Chuck E. Cheese was actually a step toward accepting that difficult part of my life. Bryan and I now have a strange fondness for that snapshot. It is bittersweet in that it represents our daughter at her most difficult phase of life—a phase we somehow survived—and yet it also reminds us of the bonding that took place as we struggled against a conflict that threatened to tear our family apart. Now that we are in a better place, we can actually look at that photo and laugh. Although I would not want to repeat that time in our lives, the way we responded helped shape our family and bring us together in a unique way.

Likewise, your family's trials will shape you and cause you to grow—for better or for worse. The challenge is to allow your trying situations to grow your family for the better. You have to learn to *accept* your "new normal" situation *and not be afraid of the hard work, persistence and faith needed to make a better tomorrow.*

I hung onto two helpful scriptures when our family was facing some dismal circumstances. The first was Galatians 6:9, in which Paul writes, "Let us not become weary in doing good, for at the proper time we will reap a harvest if we do not give up." I wrote out this verse and placed it on my bedroom dresser so I could read it when it seemed my hard work for my children was not making a difference. The second verse was John 16:33, in which Jesus states, "In me you may have peace. In this world you will have trouble. But take heart! I have overcome the world." This verse reminded me that as I went through difficulties, God could bring about a sense of peace that seemed utterly unreasonable given the circumstances. I just needed to stay connected to Him to receive the comfort, strength, and rest needed to face another day.

You are not alone in your struggles. As was the case in Joseph's situation, God still creates good out of tragedy and hope out of despair. If you are able to accept and commit your new normal life to Him, He can bring many blessings to you and to the world through you.

10. What glimmer of good do you see in your new normal situation that might bless you, your family, or the world around you?

_____

_____

_____

_____

_____

I hope you will share this thought with your child or family sometime this week and remember to add it to your Evidence of Hope Record from chapter 1.

Prayer Thought

Lord, give me wisdom, peace, and strength to move forward each day as I learn to accept my new situation and parent my special-needs child. Help me to bloom where I am planted, even though the task seems impossible at times. I recognize my own inability to fully understand the life to which I have been called, but I ask that You provide me with the understanding and peace I need to live each day with Your joy and power.

Chapter 3

WHEN GRIEF COMES TO VISIT

After months of seeking the cause of our daughter's difficulties, it was actually somewhat of a relief to discover that autism was the culprit. The time of waiting and wondering was finally over, and now at least we knew what to research, whom to call for help, and how to explain Katie's difficulties to family and friends. I threw myself into learning about treatment options and ways to implement them.

In the midst of this activity, Bryan and I had the chance to get away for an afternoon to attend a wedding. It was the first time since moving to a new state that we had left our young children with a babysitter. I remember being a bit nervous but thrilled at the chance to leave "romper room" and enter the world of grown-ups for a day. It was a beautiful wedding. The bride was radiant, her eyes shining with hope and promise, and seeing her made me reminisce about my own wedding day. Back then, life seemed perfect. The future was ours. I remembered all the dreams Bryan and I had for our lives. We were ready to take on the world with gusto.

In the midst of my reminiscing, grief hit me unexpectedly and poured over me like a flood. It struck me to the core of my soul, and the tears began to stream down my face. All my dreams were gone. Our precious baby girl had autism, and it would irreparably change the life of our entire family. In my efforts to fight against the effects of autism, I was becoming a haggard and exhausted mother, a shell of my former joyful self. I had already been grieving for Katie, but on that day I grieved for myself as well.

The grief turned into depression for at least a few months as life around me continued on as before, yet nothing was the same. Everything looked gray and dreary. On the rare date nights I had with Bryan, I found it hard to smile or engage in light discussions. How dare the world go on while my baby was hurting and my heart was broken? How dare this change my whole life as a consequence! I had plans, and dealing with autism affecting my child was not one of them.

Thanks to God's good timing, Bryan was coping better than me at the time. He was not immune to the grief, but it affected him much later, after I had finished my first wave of sadness. Most likely, his grief was delayed because he was gone ten to twelve hours each day at a new job where he was respected and in control. My job was on the home front, where I received the direct assault of the crying, tantrums, anxiety, and pain of my child. Clearly, I was not in control as I searched for solutions that were not easy to find or to implement. Of course, it was difficult for Bryan as well. He came home to an exhausted and distraught wife, and there was little chance for relaxation until the kids were in bed. Only by God's grace did we survive that period of time.

Also by the grace of God, I eventually came out of that fog of depression. I learned to laugh again and smile at the gifts God had put into my life. We began to see progress in Katie. She had delayed social language, so it was a wonderful gift when she learned to call "Mommy" from upstairs to get my attention. As she became less anxious, she began to smile more than scowl. She also began to care more about interacting with the world. For her fourth birthday, she chose a Barney cake. I can still picture her bright smile as she blew out the candles. She and her sister, Madeline, would sometimes play, hold hands, and laugh with each other. As I witnessed Katie's progress, I began to see the good once again. The worst of the grief was over, and I found it easier to tackle solutions to some of the problems.

The Phases of Grief

My situation is typical of what most people experience during the early stages of grief. After a traumatic or potentially life-altering experience, most people respond with shock, disbelief, and possibly a denial of the difficult reality. Next, they go through a phase in which they experience feelings of anger and/or guilt. I spent months wondering if I inadvertently did something during the pregnancy that harmed my child. Was it my genetic pool or the virus I contracted that caused the problem? Was it the half glass of wine I drank before I knew I was pregnant? Or could it have been the dental appointment, or the walk through the newly painted building?

Although parents of children with special needs logically know we cannot be held account-able for our genetic makeup or exposure to toxic environments that were unknown to us, we will still often feel guilt. Some of us feel guilty for not discovering the diagnosis soon enough and failing to secure treatment for our child earlier in his or her life. Or we feel we should somehow have been all-knowing to prevent any harm to our child. We can have a difficult time forgiving ourselves for being human. More importantly, we may find it difficult to believe that God's good can still prevail (recall the story of Joseph from chapter 2).

During the third stage in the grieving process, parents will typically experience feelings of depression and/or anxiety. As I mentioned, in my case this phase lasted a few months as I struggled to deal with what my and my family's life would look like now that Katie had been diagnosed with autism. During the final phase of this typical grief pattern, parents may gain some acceptance of the situation and initiate more action-oriented problem-solving activities.

Note that the phases of grief may affect each of your family members at *different times*. As I shared earlier, my husband was coping better than I was when I hit my first wave of depression. He was at his workplace much of the time and was sheltered from the daily onslaught of difficulties, so I think it was easier for him to remain in the denial phase for a longer period of time. Of course, he eventually also felt the full brunt of our daughter's disability and went through the other phases of grief—just later than me. When the sadness was really affecting him, I was already deep into the problem-solving phase of coping.

While it was tempting for me to be frustrated that he was stuck in the sadness phase while I had moved on to problem solving, it was important for me to recognize that his stages of grieving were on a different time schedule than mine. We each had to experience the different phases in our own time. As I mentioned, this was probably God's good timing, because at least one of us was feeling relatively upbeat and energetic while the other was discouraged.

The stages of grief will also affect siblings, grandparents, and other close family members at different times. Family members who do not live in the same geographical area may have an especially hard time accepting the fact that their niece, nephew, grandson, or granddaughter has a significant problem. Because they may only see our child in small doses and in vacation settings, they likely won't see the problems clearly. In addition, it is not uncommon for extended family members to suspect the parents to be the cause of the problem. As the parents adjust their parenting techniques to what seems to work best for their child, others in the family might view these approaches as spoiling, coddling, or alternately, stressful or over-demanding for the child.

We will address this specific problem in greater detail in chapter 7, but for now the take-home point is that friends and family members will "get" our children's issues in their own time. As parents, we can educate them on the problems, but we have to realize that some will be slower to understand and that they will have their own grief cycles. At any given time, one family member might be struggling with depression or anxiety while another will be in complete denial of the diagnosis. This is especially problematic when we want to reach out for support, and they respond by questioning why we are so upset over what they believe is a minor situation. While this is infuriating, we will cope much better if we recognize their current level of understanding and are patient with them as they work through their own phase of grieving.

1. What loss or disappointment are you grieving now?

   _____

   _____

   _____

2. What stage of grief are you in now (denial, anger, guilt, depression or action)?

   _____

   _____

   _____

3. Is another family member (such as a spouse, other children, or grandparents) in a different stage of grief than you at this time? If so, which stage?

   _____

   _____

   _____

4. How has this affected you?

   _____

   _____

   _____

Hosting the Return Visitor

The part that is sometimes missed in the discussion of grief is that it can return to visit you more often than you think. I remember feeling irritated at myself more than once for returning to sadness after I had moved on to the action and problem-solving phase of the grief process. Over the years, I had developed many skills for helping my daughter, and I tried to put on my professional hat and respond with logic to each new crisis. I had already gone through the depressive phase, and I wanted to stuff down any new feelings of sadness so I could better attend to the business of coordinating and supervising Katie's therapy. What I didn't know is that grief has a frequent-flier program. I thought I knew all there was to know about this particular visitor. I had spent plenty of time in its company, and I believed I could no longer benefit from its presence. Nevertheless, it kept showing up on my doorstep.

Grief revisited our family in an intense way when Katie was ten-years-old, long after the initial diagnosis and initial phases of grief. It was late December, and Katie was playing a game in a city basketball league. Although Bryan and I knew it could be extremely difficult for her to play fast-moving competitive games like basketball, she loved the sport, and we were proud of her willingness to try. We had been working with her to help her remain as calm as possible during intense moments, and we were hoping and praying for the best. After the game, we planned to celebrate Christmas within our immediate family, as we would be visiting relatives on Christmas Day.

Our plans quickly changed when disaster struck. At one point in the game, Katie perceived that one small girl had fouled her several times, and she suddenly pushed her down. Katie was much larger than this girl, so her actions looked especially bad. I sank down in my seat, aghast and embarrassed, and tried to determine what I should do. Should I let the coaches handle it? Should I rush down to the court? I didn't have much time to think, as the girl's mother quickly leapt from her seat and yelled throughout the echoing gymnasium, "Get that girl out of here! She's out of control!"

I was horrified. Of course, the officials stopped the game as the coaches helped the girl up and assessed the situation. I quickly walked down to meet Katie off the court. Several conflicting thoughts were swirling through my mind. Who was I more upset with—my daughter or the screaming mother? My daughter's behavior was certainly wrong and deserved consequences, but did that mother really have to make such a loud and rude public response? Had no other child ever pushed someone during a game? Did all the parents in the gym feel like this mother? What were they thinking about our family? I tried not to make eye contact with anyone as I made my way down, as I didn't think I could handle any more rejection.

I reached the court and tried to inconspicuously rush my daughter outside to calm her down. The other girl was not hurt, but her mother was furious. I was completely humiliated. I had hardly ever broken a rule in my life, and here was my daughter publicly establishing herself as the fifth-grade basketball bully.

Outside, I chastised Katie with a heavy heart and then told her she needed to apologize to the girl. We returned inside, where I apologized to the mother and attempted to explain Katie's disability. I was hoping to raise some level of compassion or understanding in her, but the mother was so focused on what had just happened to her child that she was not able to hear me.

No one offered us any consolation. It wasn't that we expected it or deserved it, but it certainly would have helped. Katie looked like any other girl her age, and nobody understood her sensory sensitivities and inner struggles to maintain calm. Nobody knew her anxiety or our heartache and how hard we all tried to manage her autism. Nobody knew all the years of teaching and coaching we had done for her to even be able to play the game. All they knew was that my child was the kid who lost it.

Tears streamed down my face as we made our way home, but I held back the sobs so I could drive safely and keep Katie calm. Needless to say, our Christmas celebration was seriously dampened that evening. The next day, we received a phone call from the league asking Katie not to return. We considered fighting the decision and asking for support because of Katie's disability, but ultimately decided the strict consequence might serve as a teaching tool. Our fighting spirit had also been killed by our desire to avoid more misunderstanding and pain. This compilation of unfortunate events intensified our grief.

I realize other families have experienced more traumatic incidents than we have. Some homes are filled with ongoing verbal or physical violence that makes pushing seem mild. I know of one child who threw knives at her father during a bipolar mixed-manic episode. I also know a mom who carries a physical scar from an object her child threw at her during a rage. Parents have driven their children to emergency rooms for a suicide watch, all the while hoping the child would not jump out of the moving car en route. Lives have been permanently altered due to substance abuse in a family. However, while our basketball story might seem mild in comparison, it was still difficult for us, and we struggled to feel joyous that Christmas.

Coping with Returning Grief

Katie's basketball episode illustrates why grief tends to return to us long after the initial shock of the diagnosis has passed. As our child moves through each stage of development, we again experience grief when we see him or her suffer from being behind, or on a different schedule, or just out of sync with others. Even if months or years have passed since our child's disability was identified, the grief will hit again when those disabilities present themselves in a new way.

This renewed feeling of sadness might occur when we see our child engage in inappropriate behavior, as was the case with my daughter's actions during the basketball game. It can arise when we watch children without disabilities perform academically, athletically, artistically, or socially with little difficulty. It can be triggered when we hear parents talk about their child's achievements. It can revisit us when we attend student award ceremonies, even if our child is one of the award recipients. As happy as we are that our child is being honored, it can make us emotional to realize how much hard work had to take place for him or her to achieve that honor, compared to the kids for whom success comes more easily. Grief can also return when people misunderstand our child's disability and assume he or she is spoiled, lazy, or rude. These judgments are hard for us to take as parents, and we feel a sense of rejection. Even worse is watching our child be rejected.

Tom and Sue, two friends of mine, have a daughter named Amy who has learning disabilities and social challenges. Amy often played with Megan, the neighbor girl, as they were close in age and lived two houses apart. They were not best friends, but they enjoyed one another as neighbor kids often do. One day, Tom and Sue were invited to the neighbor's house for a chat. When they arrived, the neighbors told them that they should discourage Amy from getting too attached to Megan, because Megan would eventually "move on" and leave Amy behind. While Tom and Sue knew the girls would grow apart one day, it was a harsh proclamation to receive over a cup of coffee. Yet they listened calmly and tried to be "neighborly" in their responses. Later, when my friend was alone in her bedroom, she cried the tears that came about as a result of the already planned rejection of her child.

As I mentioned, it can be frustrating to be in a problem-solving mode when feelings of sadness from the earlier stages of grief reappear. In my own situation, I did not feel I had the time or energy to keep bursting into tears. I wanted to be done with this stage of the process. However, as much as I wished it away, the reality was that I had to acknowledge and deal with it each time it showed up.

During this process, I learned it is necessary for parents to accept the sadness that returns and allow themselves to grieve beyond the period they initially thought they would. As long as they are still able to carry out their functions as parents, the grieving process will foster healing within them and bring them closer to accepting their new normal. Over time, the grief will visit less frequently and stay a shorter period of time, and parents will learn greater acceptance and be strengthened to help others. More importantly, they will become better able to help their challenged child when he or she begins to grieve.

5. What situations in your life have triggered grief to return when you felt you were past this stage? How do you feel about the return of that stage of grief?

_____

_____

_____

_____

6. What have you learned from these return visits from grief? In what ways do you feel stronger and more equipped to face the situation in the future?

_____

_____

_____

When Grief Visits Your Challenged Child

As you may have already experienced, grief over social, emotional or behavioral difficulties will not only visit you and your family members, but it will also visit your affected child. For many, this grief is triggered when your child's attempts to make friends are snubbed, or when he or she perceives they are missing out on what the other kids are doing. These events can leave your child feeling isolated, lonely and wishing they could be different. Complicating the problem is the fact that you might be so caught up in your own pain that you forget to look at the world from your child's perspective and remember he or she grieves over the disabilities just as you do.

Grieving might look different in children, so as a parent, you need to be attuned to the signs. When children begin to learn they have a disability—or sense they are different—they may act out, deny they have any problems, or blame their problems on others. This may last for months or even years, as children are usually slower to assimilate what the disability means and how to cope with it. When they enter the anger phase, they may lash out at you, the caregiver, because you are "safe" to them and they know you will love them unconditionally. This grief behavior may be in addition to the social, emotional, or behavior challenges your child already experiences.

Although I was not the source of my daughter's pain, when we decided to try homeschooling Katie at age eleven, the first few months were characterized by her yelling—at me. Although it was difficult for me to endure, I knew that she was feeling pain and that she was not able to speak to me rationally at the time. She knew I truly loved her unconditionally and that I would not reject her if she released her grief, anger, and frustration on me. We persevered, and later she did learn to express her grief in more appropriate ways.

It is important to be aware that children also express depression differently than adults and older teens. While adults usually become lethargic, unmotivated and appear sad, depressed children may become aggressive, disobedient, and irritable. As a parent, it is important for you to realize this may be a normal part of their grieving process. Your child will not have the experience to know that circumstances always change and often get better, so he or she might be more impulsive than an adult and make foolish decisions. For this reason, while you can be a sounding board and source of unconditional love, it is wise to seek medical help and/or professional counseling for a child dealing with depression or grief. It is a painful process, and your child will need all the help that is available.

7. What are some things that might be causing your child to grieve right now?

_____

_____

_____

8. What stage of grief do you think he or she is experiencing?

_____

_____

_____

Answering the Tough Questions

Watching a child suffer physically, emotionally, or spiritually is one of the most painful things a parent can endure. It raises tough questions that have no easy answers. I remember the heart-wrenching sadness and anger I felt toward God at different times during Katie's development. I would often cry out, "God, why us? Why autism?" Autism seemed an especially horrible disability because it robbed my daughter of one of the greatest joys of living: the ability to build deep friendships. It impaired her social intuition and kept many friendship skills just beyond her grasp. How could God create her to want companionship and then allow her disability to deprive her of this basic human need? And why were His people failing to love and befriend her in the way they should? Why were her Christian peers not reaching out to my precious child?

Although I had learned to trust God, I did not understand how any of this suffering was producing anything good. I really wanted some answers. Then, somewhere in the re-grieving process, God impressed upon my heart that He knew how I felt. He led me to verses such as Isaiah 53:3, which foretells a suffering Savior who "was despised and rejected by men, a man of sorrows, and familiar with suffering," and Hebrews 5:8-9, which states Jesus suffered as we do and can sympathize with our troubles because He was fully a man. As I read these passages, *it struck me that God felt the same pain* when He watched His Son suffer as I did when I watched my daughter suffer. However, unlike me, He could have changed the situation and eased His Son's pain, but out of love for you and me, He chose not to do so.

This thought was a turning point for me—it helped me understand that God and Jesus knew *fully* what I was experiencing. I also began to comprehend for the first time the depth of God's love for me. At the cross, He was willing to allow His Son to suffer temporary—but excruciating—pain because He knew it was our only hope. While He knew Jesus' suffering would end and He would live happily for eternity, He still had to watch the pain and allow it to happen because it was the only way to fulfill His good plan of salvation for us.

When Jesus came to earth as a human, He experienced the full extent of physical, emotional, and spiritual pain that humans feel. You may or may not have experienced close and loving friends turn away from you in your hour of need, but Jesus endured this pain on the night that He was betrayed. In the Garden of Gethsemane on the night before His death, Jesus said to His friends, the disciples, "My soul is overwhelmed with sorrow to the point of death. Stay here and keep watch with me" (Matthew 26:38). But none of them were willing or able to stay awake and pray with Him. Later, when the pressure became intense, Peter, Jesus' supposedly good friend, denied that he even knew his Lord.

As I reflected on Jesus' crucifixion, I realized how selfish it was of me to think my family should be exempt from pain when even the all-powerful Creator of the universe went through times of suffering. While I do not know if Katie has experienced this same revelation, she has been increasingly able to accept her disability, talk about it, ask for help, see her limitations, and even laugh at herself. This progress is nothing short of miraculous, considering that at one time her sadness was so deep that she regretted even living.

Accepting Pain

The similarity between my human suffering and God's divine suffering leads me to another key point in maintaining our mental health while raising a challenged child: that is, *to accept that pain is just a part of living in this world and that no family is exempt.* This understanding helps move us from the pity phase of grief into the arena where we can be of more help to our family and others. While it does not make the pain disappear, it does make it seem less strange and unfair.

In Ecclesiastes 9:11 we read that time and chance happen to all. Nobody is exempt from pain. Sometimes our personal pain will seem unbearable, but we are not to give up! I like the way Paul encouraged the believers in Corinth when he said that though their troubles seemed all-consuming, they should "not lose heart" because their troubles were achieving an eternal glory that made it all worth it (see 2 Corinthians 4:16-17). Paul knew that pain would give them a greater opportunity to appreciate the relief of grace that comes from the risen Jesus Christ—a grace that would last forever. While this may sound trite to you, I can honestly say that though I would not have chosen my children to have neurological problems, I would not give up the relationship with God that resulted as He led us through the pain.

God's Comfort

Although there is a long-term purpose for pain, God does not leave us without comfort in our short-term troubles. He sent the Holy Spirit, known as the Comforter (see John 14:16, KJV) so we would not be alone in our suffering. He also reminds us that one day our pain will cease. As Jesus told His disciples, "Now is your time of grief, but I will see you again and you will rejoice, and no one will take away your joy" (John 16:22).

I must admit that the mom in me still wants to protect my children from pain and suffering. However, my growing desire is to teach my children that God allows pain to accomplish His greater purposes through us. These greater purposes include an increased compassion and understanding for others as we work through our own struggles. Because of our experience with suffering and God's comfort, we are able to help others during their trials (see 2 Corinthians 1:4). We are able to understand what they are going through in a way that no person with a seemingly "perfect" and carefree life can do. I know that in my own life, those who have most inspired me are people who have experienced serious trials and turned to God for help. I am drawn to their God-given wisdom and peace. In the same way, God's big picture is to draw others to Himself as the peace-giver and the author/provider of eternal life.

Another problem that plagues parents of socially, emotionally, or behaviorally challenged children is that we may feel we have received a greater portion of suffering than others, and we wonder why. Job asked God this question when he experienced great trials. After God's response, Job ultimately had to admit that God's reasons and ways were "too wonderful" for him "to know" (see Job 42:3). Similarly, Isaiah 55:9 tells us that God's thoughts are higher than our thoughts and that His ways are higher than our (human) ways. We cannot even fathom how God might manage all the details of universe. If we are to find peace, we have to be humble enough to accept this.

In the end we have a choice. We can choose to trust God and make the best of our circumstances. We can also choose to compete with God's omnipotence and be continually questioning, miserable, and whiny. We may not like it, but in the absence of being able to control every situation, it is best to seek to be a blessing to others in spite of our circumstances.

9. In what ways have those who have endured serious trials been a source of strength and comfort to you?

_____

_____

_____

10. In what ways do you think God can likewise use the pain you have endured to fulfill His purpose of showing love to the world?

_____

_____

_____

11. What are some areas in your life that you need to concede to God's omnipotence so you can experience peace and be a greater blessing to others?

_____

_____

_____

Gaining Joy and Peace

When I look back on my family's Christmas basketball escapade, I realize the joy and peace I could have experienced if I had focused on the truth of what Christmas actually represents—that Christ came into the world to take away all the pain, humiliation, and hopelessness I was feeling that night. Jesus is the reason why a disabled child and her haggard mother can have hope in a lost and out-of-control world. The wonderful gift that disability gives us is that we are not held hostage to the lie that this world is all there is and there is nothing better to come. Instead, we are intimately aware of the pain and imperfection this world brings and look eagerly to heaven as our home.

But do we have to wait to go to heaven to experience God's peace? Thankfully, the answer is no. When Jesus announced, "The kingdom of heaven has come upon you" (Matthew 12:28), it meant His presence would now allow people to experience a piece of heaven on earth. Jesus was the fulfillment of mankind's hope for eternal joy, and by acknowledging that Jesus is the center of our lives, we can get a sneak preview of that joy. By coming to earth, dying, and being resurrected, Jesus conquered death and all that would hold us prisoner to sin and sadness, so we do not have to wait until we die or Christ returns to earth to experience some of the peace and joy that heaven offers.

Of course, the complete fulfillment of heaven is yet to come, for we will only experience perfect fellowship with God when we are resurrected at Christ's return. However, through prayer and His Word, we can have constant communication with the author of hope, love, and peace. This communication will transform our minds (see Romans 12:2) so we are better able to see life as He sees it. Our challenge is to allow God's kingdom to reign in our hearts, which means turning our grief over to Him and learning to see life from His eternal perspective. Relinquishing control can be difficult, but it is safe because Jesus is our Prince of Peace (see Isaiah 9:6), and He is faithful and true (see Revelation 19:11).

> Our challenge is to allow God's kingdom to reign in our hearts, which means turning our grief over to Him and learning to see life from His eternal perspective.

12. In what ways have you experienced the kingdom of heaven on earth? In other words, how have you experienced God's joy and peace in the midst of pain?

_____

_____

_____

Do Not Be Afraid

Of course, as we go through the grieving process, we still have practical tasks to accomplish. We have to help our children get the appropriate education, therapy, and whatever else they need. But as we run around trying to drum up good services for our children, we would benefit from following the advice Moses gave to the Hebrews when they stood on the shore of the Red Sea. Hemmed in by the Egyptian army on one side and the sea on the other, the Hebrews seemed to be on the brink of destruction. But Moses, filled with a mind transformed by faith in God, said to them, "Do not be afraid. Stand firm and you will see the deliverance the LORD will bring you today. The Egyptians you see today you will never see again. The LORD will fight for you; you need only to be still." (Exodus 14:13-14). In the same way, we need to learn to keep our hearts "still" and peaceful, even as our bodies move into action. We need to stand firm in our relationship with Christ and watch for God's deliverance. It will come!

13. Write the first two sentences in Exodus 14:13 in the space below.

_____

_____

_____

14. What would it look like on a daily basis if you were to incorporate these words into your life?

_____

_____

_____

Prayer Thought

Lord, You know that my child and I are suffering, and today I ask for Your grace. Help us not only survive the pain but also overcome in the way Jesus did, by fulfilling Your purpose on earth. Thank You for Your infinite wisdom. Although I don't always comprehend Your purpose and plan in every situation, I trust that You are in control and that You work all things together for good. Please help me to bear my pain in a manner that brings good to others and glory to You each day.

Chapter 4

LEARNING THE JOB YOU NEVER WANTED

I CAN'T DO THIS!" I yelled out to my mother, choking back the tears. My mom had come all the way from California to Kentucky to visit the grandkids and offer support to me, a struggling mom in a new home with no close friends or family nearby. I was at the beginning of my special-needs journey, and I was overwhelmed with the responsibility of taking care of two difficult young children. Adding to these feelings of isolation and frustration were the new jobs I had to undertake. Once Katie's diagnosis of autism had been confirmed, a new season of life had begun for us. Accepting the diagnosis was hard enough, but taking the time and energy to learn the techniques to actually help our daughter was an even bigger challenge.

The diagnosis launched me into a season of research. Due to a general lack of understanding of autism at the time, I needed to overcome a steep learning curve so I could grasp the world of autism treatment. The work I did was both an emotional and an academic experience. I envied those who could read these books and have only a professional interest, for often what I read would move me to tears. Yet I plowed through them to glean any information that might help Katie. There were almost no how-to therapy books for autism available, so I had to read between the lines to pick up ideas. When I could not sleep at night, I would get up and study, taking copious notes of techniques I could try with Katie in the coming weeks.

The real problem began after I realized what needed to be done. The research indicated that Katie had to be immersed in structured play, activity, and conversation almost every waking hour. My husband was gone long hours at a new job, so planning and implementing this type of therapy was up to me. There were no autism early intervention programs where we lived, so I had to constantly engage Katie to keep her from retreating into her own little world. This meant I spent a lot of floor time with her and other playmates who came to the house. As I mentioned earlier, to accomplish this, I took time off from working on my doctoral degree.

I cannot honestly say that my daughter appreciated the work I was doing. My efforts were met with frequent tears and attempts to disengage from the activity. It was exhausting. Although I loved my daughter, I never wanted to be a preschool teacher or a special education teacher. But there I was, a committed stay-at-home mom in a new community and the main playmate and teacher for my child.

My cry of insufficiency to my mother stemmed from my exhaustion in trying to be the perfect mother and therapist. It also developed out of a fear that my efforts might fail, dooming my daughter to a less-than-adequate life. Although my mother firmly encouraged me that I could do this job, I didn't believe it. I did not think I could handle the physical and emotional loads. I had faced and overcome many difficulties in the past, but this one seemed *so* much bigger than me. I had little faith in my ability to survive this trial and retain mental health within the family.

The Impact of Inadequacy

It was then that I began to question God's choice of entrusting this child to me. Although I considered myself to be a fairly capable person, I found myself feeling incompetent for this new job. It seemed my daughter would have been better served with a naturally playful mom who loved nothing more than engaging in silly children's games and activities. This was just not me. I was an intellectual type of person who was most comfortable in a university setting of graduate students. Caring for Katie meant I constantly had to force myself to be an outgoing preschool activity coordinator. Often I just wanted to shut myself into my bedroom and read a good book, but this was not the season for such activity.

Once again my situation is not unique. All parents with a special-needs child have to do research and learn new jobs—some of which they never had any desire to master. Some parents have to learn sign language or Braille. Some have to learn to give injections or change ostomy bags. Others have to learn physical or occupational therapy techniques to do with their child. Those who have children with social, emotional, or behavioral challenges have to become behavior-modification specialists. They may need to become home educators for academic and social training and interpreters of the world for their children who, for a variety of reasons, see life differently.

1. In what ways have you felt overwhelmed or unqualified to handle the challenges of raising your child with social, emotional, or behavioral challenges?

    _____

    _____

    _____

God's Response

As parents, few of us feel ready for these jobs when they are thrust upon us, but we have little choice in learning them—even if they leave us feeling incompetent and exhausted. Thankfully, we are not the first to feel unqualified or overwhelmed (nor will we be the last). In the Bible, we read many stories of people who felt the same way.

Both Moses and Gideon, for example, felt completely unqualified for the jobs God had designed for them. They even had reasonable excuses as to why their lack of talent or status should disqualify them. In Exodus 4, Moses told God that he could not lead the people because of his speech impediment. One would have to agree that a person with a stuttering problem might not be the best candidate to speak with a world leader, but God chose him anyway.

In Judges 6, we learn that Gideon came from the weakest clan and he was the least respected in his family. His lack of heroic qualities would seem to make him a poor choice for leading God's troops into battle, but God did not excuse him. Apparently, God knew something about both Moses and Gideon that qualified them for the jobs He wanted them to do. So He told them both not to worry, for He would be with them. When they still lacked courage, He sent someone with technical and/or moral support (Aaron and Purah, respectively) to help with the tasks.

With that exhortation and offer of help, Moses and Gideon did the best they could and relied on God to fill in the gaps. Of course, they had the advantage of knowing their new jobs were God ordained. God spoke directly to Moses through a burning bush, and He provided Gideon with several miracles to confirm his call. We rarely get our call in such a supernatural way—most of us are chosen by birthing and loving our child and then having the special-needs bomb dropped on us later without any training, warning, or bunker in which to hide. However, in retrospect we can often see how God was preparing us ahead of time for the task.

At the time of my special-needs crash course, I had no specific belief that God had called me to this job. Like Moses and Gideon, I was unable to see how I could do it well. I did the best I could, but I was constantly concerned that I was not the perfect mother-therapist. At first I did not have anyone to help me, nor did I expect God to fill in the gaps—I pretty much relied on myself for the strength and wisdom I needed. This was my spiritual immaturity in action. I kept thinking that if I worked hard enough, as I always had, I would figure out this new normal. Instead, all of my efforts just led to exhaustion.

Handing Off the Burden

One day, I had finally had enough! I felt as if I had been carrying ten bowling balls around my neck for several months, and the burden finally was so overwhelming I had to set it down. I remember sitting down on my dining room floor, which had been converted to the children's playroom. There were toys scattered across the carpet, dirty dishes filling the sink, and laundry piling up. There was a mess all around me, but it was nothing compared to the emotional mess I had become.

I rested my elbows on the little wooden toddler table, placed my face in my hands, and wept. "God," I cried, "please help me. I can't do this anymore." At that moment, a miracle occurred. Then and there I felt the weight lift from my shoulders. To this day I cannot fully explain it. I just knew that I was no longer alone in the battle and that God was there to help. Of course, He had been there the moment the difficulty began, but for me to accept that help, I had to come to the end of my self-reliant and stoic self. It was a difficult but beautiful day when I recognized my insufficiency and was ready to submit to Him. From that moment on, God began to teach me that He was in control and I could trust Him.

When I woke up the next day, the fatigue and challenges with my children had not miraculously disappeared. Mary Poppins did not swoop in to whip the children into shape and fix up the house. Moses did not arrive to set me free. However, God gave me a renewed strength and motivation to make a few phone calls to look for some part-time preschool or babysitting help. It was such a small thing, and yet so powerful!

Within a few hours, I had the name of a woman who was just starting a new Christian preschool. The class was small and organized, making it a perfect fit for Katie. It soon became clear to me that I had received this technical help and support from God the moment I had recognized my weakness and turned to His provision. I realized how I had been trying to do everything by myself when all along the powerful God of the universe was there to offer His help.

2. What "impossible" tasks are you facing today that could be put into God's hands?

_____

_____

_____

Wonderful Weaknesses

Before these difficult tasks I faced with parenting my child, I must say that I had never considered my weaknesses to be wonderful in any way. However, in 2 Corinthians 12:9, Paul writes that God told him, "My grace is sufficient for you, for *my power is made perfect in weakness*" (emphasis added). This is an amazing statement. Our weakness can actually aid God's purposes so that His grace is seen more clearly in us.

If you are like me you might find this hard to grasp. Somewhere in life, I had learned that weaknesses should be identified and then eliminated with hard work. I had carried this mindset into my role as a parent, and I worked hard to overcome (or at least hide) my flaws so I could be who I thought I needed to be for my children. While it was good for me to recognize my weaknesses, I know now it was wrong for me to be so critical of myself. It was sinful for me to reject the person God created me to be—a person, like you, who was created "to do good works, which God prepared in advance for us to do" (Ephesians 2:10). As our Creator, God knows our strengths and weaknesses better than we do. I was wrong in believing that good could come only from my strengths.

In Psalm 139:14, God tells us we are "fearfully and wonderfully made." We have each been uniquely built for His specific purposes. Just because the task we face is difficult does not mean it has not been ordained for us. In fact, God has made a habit of asking His people to do seemingly *impossible* things! He asked Joshua to knock down the walls of Jericho by playing trumpets (see Joshua 6). He enabled a shepherd boy named David to kill the giant Goliath with a few stones (see 1 Samuel 17). In the New Testament, Jesus asked His followers to feed 4,000 people with seven fish and a few loaves of bread (see Matthew 15:32-39; Mark 8:1-9). He enabled His disciples to heal diseases and cast out unclean spirits (see Matthew 10; Mark 6:6-13; Luke 9:1-6).

By asking us to do what seems impossible, God stretches us and helps us learn to rely on Him alone. Not only does He then help us accomplish the task He has given, but He also takes our weaknesses and shows the world *His* power and sufficiency through them. This is God's specialty, and He has been doing it throughout the ages with amazing results.

Again, God's dealings with Gideon provide a perfect example of how this works. In Judges 7:3, God told Gideon to *decrease* the size of his army before invading the Midianites so it would be clear the victory came from God and not from Israel's strength. One would think God would bless Israel by increasing the size or strength of its troops, but He did just the opposite. In fact, two times He asked Gideon to dismiss some of his soldiers, so that his army went from 30,000 men to just 300 men. By doing this, God purposely weakened the Israelite forces, which was probably quite frightening for Gideon.

God must have realized how impossible this strategy would have seemed to Gideon, because He went on to provide moral support. He sent Gideon and Purah to the Midianite camp in the middle of the night, where the two overheard a soldier relate his dream to a friend. This friend interpreted the dream as a sign of sure victory for Israel, which was enough to inspire Gideon to act as the mighty warrior God knew he was. He led the Israelite army to an amazing victory in spite of its small size.

By all accounts, Gideon's initial lack of confidence and his small army were weaknesses, but they were no problem for God. Clearly, our spiritual strength is much more important to God than any superpower we might wish to gain.

Handling Our Weakness

The situations we are facing might not be as dramatic as those of Gideon or Moses. However, they can help us learn to accept our weaknesses and recognize that God has allowed them for a purpose. We can be certain that God will fill in the gaps if we ask Him—or He will allow our weaknesses to continue in order to strengthen us spiritually. His sovereignty in this area allows us freedom to be ourselves, the people God created us to be, flaws and all. We can use our strengths to His glory, and He can use our weaknesses "perfectly" to His glory as well (see 2 Corinthians 12:9). As with everything else God has given us, even our weaknesses are a gift from above. Wow! Who but God could turn our worst characteristics into a glorious display of His splendor?

God encourages us to take our problems to Him in prayer, and He blesses us when we allow Him to answer them in His sufficiency and through His grace. God's answers may not always be the easiest or best solutions we have in our mind—and sometimes the answer will involve hard work and will stretch our capabilities—but His ways are always sufficient and always push us in the right direction.

If we look back on our past, we will see how God knows our strengths and weaknesses and uses them to guide our development. I love how in Judges 6:12, the angel of the Lord saw the potential in Gideon and called him a "mighty warrior," even though Gideon did not have this opinion of himself. As with Gideon, God realizes the potential in us that we cannot see. We may sometimes feel He is stretching us to the breaking point, but He is actually training us in those areas where we need to learn to trust and depend on Him. If we never reached a place where our weaknesses compelled us to cry out to God for help, it would be more difficult for us to know Him deeply and trust Him. God shows His strength in these situations so we can take part in that strength and share it with others.

> God realizes the potential in us that we cannot see.

48

God has revealed His strength to me through my weaknesses and has taught me to give thanks even for my shortcomings. In fact, one of the ways He strengthened me in spite of my human weaknesses was in the writing of this book. In the months leading up to the genesis of this book, I had less time and energy for speaking engagements and involvement in the non-profit organization I founded. I disliked this need for extra rest as I perceived myself as weak and less capable than I would have liked to be. However, over time, it caused me to wonder if God was keeping me home for a reason. It was then that I began to reflect on the stories and principles outlined in this book, which I had been experiencing and meditating upon for more than fifteen years. I realized this was something I could do to communicate God's hope to others in a way that conserved my energy. Instead of having to put on a sharp suit and work up a perky routine for an audience, I could write in a cluttered room in my pajamas and sip a cup of tea.

God chose the perfect time for me to write down what He had taught me. He took my physical weakness and used it for His glory and my good. I don't know that I ever would have written this book had I been given the energy for my choice of activities. If God could do something worthwhile with my chronic fatigue, just think what He could do with our other weaknesses as flawed moms and dads.

3. What weaknesses in your life could God have ordained in order to increase your spiritual strength?

    _____

    _____

4. How do you feel about this "wonderful weakness"?

    _____

    _____

    _____

Stupendous Strengths

In addition to using our weaknesses, God will use our strengths to achieve His purposes. In my own life, what I lacked in childlike energy was compensated for by my intuition of what my child needed to learn and my determination to provide it. Soon after Katie's diagnosis, I trained several college students to work with my daughter to expand her language, coping abilities, and play skills. Almost all of these former trainees have gone on to work professionally with children with special needs. In this way, they are blessing other families as much as they blessed mine.

Later, I used the passion and skills God gave me to set up Successful Living with Autism through Training and Education (SLATE), a non-profit program, which provides social/emotional training to children with autism and gives support to their families. This program is now funded by the Department of Disability Services in the state of California and serves more than 100 children and their families each year. Although I never would have planned to accomplish these tasks earlier in my life, I believe that creating SLATE and writing this book were ordained for me as they so perfectly fit who I am and what I value. As I was going through this trial of disability in my family, God was also preparing a new vision for my life. Where I saw only the end of my life as I knew it, God saw the beginning of something better and more beautiful.

5. What are the strengths God has given you for the task of raising your child? What strengths has He given you to help others as they go through this process?

_____

_____

_____

Qualified by the Creator

Just as in my situation, God knows your weaknesses and strengths and will qualify you for the tasks He puts in front of you. Your skills and inadequacies are unique to the perfect *you* that He has created. Your child's needs are not a surprise to God, and if you walk in faith with Him, He will amaze you with all the ways He uses the strong and weak parts of you to love your child.

My teenage daughter, Madeline, recently said to me, "Mom, God picked you as the *perfect* person to be our mom." In light of my previous doubts about my fitness for motherhood, her statement was a powerful testimony to God's wisdom and a sincere encouragement to me. It also confirmed the main principle that I want you to take away from this chapter: *If God, our Creator, calls us to a*

If God calls us to a task, He will qualify us to fulfill it.

50

task, He will qualify us to fulfill it. There is no need to fret over our inabilities when God calls us to do something, because He will give us what we need to complete it.

Clearly, God's priority in our lives is not to make things easy for us, but to show us His love and power. In our difficult situations, He promises to always be with us (see Hebrews 13:5), to equip us (see Hebrews 13:20-21), and to love us and our child (see Romans 8:38-39). Our challenge is to learn to see from God's vantage point so we are willing and able to carry out the tasks He sets before us. Even if we never wanted these jobs, we can be victorious when we allow God to lead us through them.

6. As you look back on your life, in what ways has God provided for you and your family in spite of your lack of ability or resources?

_____

_____

_____

7. In Philippians 1:6, Paul tells us that "he who began a good work in you will carry it on to completion until the day of Christ Jesus." In Ephesians 2:10, he writes, "We are God's workmanship, created in Christ Jesus to do good works, which God prepared in advance for us to do." What do these verses tell you about God and His plans for you and your child?

_____

_____

_____

8. What support do these verses give you as you make decisions for your child?

_____

_____

_____

_____

Prayer Thought

Lord, thank You for the strengths You have provided to me. May I use them to further Your purposes and bring You glory. Thank You also for my weaknesses, which You are using to allow me to see Your grace at work in my life. Today, I pray that You will give me wisdom and contentment to rest in Your sufficiency.

God's Provisions for My Weaknesses

In this chapter, you may have identified some weak areas where you need God to provide His strength. In the space below, write down when and in what way God provides strength or compensates for these weaknesses in your life. Also remember to add these provisions to your Evidence of Hope Record from chapter 1.

_____

_____

_____

_____

_____

_____

_____

Chapter 5

THE REAL INSANITY: STIGMA, SHAME, AND SILENCE

Have you gone through a period of months that seemed especially difficult for you as a parent? I found myself in that place several years ago. At the time I had been home-schooling Katie for about a year. As I mentioned previously, it was a difficult job, but I pushed myself to continue because I believed it was beneficial for my daughter. At the same time I was trying to improve the health of Madeline, my third-grader, who was often sick and struggling with what seemed like hypoglycemia.

One day, I was in the grocery store looking for healthy foods for Madeline to eat. It was a bit of a thankless task, as she was a picky eater and it was likely she would refuse whatever I chose. Nevertheless, I began to engage in a debate with myself, trying to find a food that was the right combination of nutrients, but also one my daughter would actually eat. There were many choices, but none of the foods seemed like the right combination.

As I stood there debating the snack options, I pondered how much time I had spent as a mother doing this same thing in other areas of my life. I was *always* weighing the pros and cons of a situation, trying to figure out the right combination of school, therapy, diet, and other activities that would help my children. There was never one perfect choice, and some of the decisions were agonizing because they seemed to be so important to my children's welfare.

Although the snack choice was not one of these critical decisions, it proved to be the straw that broke this camel's back. Suddenly, the pressure of all these decisions came crashing down on me, and I found myself crying right there in front of a selection of energy bars. I had been under severe stress for months—years, actually—but this event finally prompted me to take a trip to the doctor for help. When I went to see her she suggested an antidepressant. I took her recommendation, and I soon felt better. I was able to continue on and handle the multiple stressors and decisions a bit more gracefully.

Later, I shared this story with a group of homeschooling moms. One of these mothers had admitted to being depressed, and I thought she might benefit from hearing the story of how I broke down in the snack food aisle. I empathized with her situation and was trying to help her feel understood—and I thought she might find the story humorous as well. But after I shared, one of the other moms looked at me with disgust and bellowed, "Wow, that's bad!" No one else in the group said a word. An awkward silence loomed, and I felt the stigma.

As you might imagine, since that time I have been more cautious with whom I share my personal struggles and setbacks. Had I shared about tripping over the shopping cart in the frozen food aisle, the response likely would have been sympathy or friendly laughter. Why was this situation so different? Did the woman consider me weak or disgusting? Based on her reaction, that's certainly how I felt.

To Speak or Not to Speak?

This story illustrates another difficulty of raising a child with social, emotional, or behavioral difficulties: such challenges can be hard to talk about. There are at least two reasons for this. If you talk about your child's special needs, people may give you unsolicited advice that you already know or is way off base. Or, alternately, you might get the response I received—people look shocked or uncomfortable, and you feel you and your child are now lower on their scale of acceptability. As you receive these responses, sometimes it is tempting to just remain silent about such problems. However, as we will discuss later in this chapter, stigma, shame, and our resulting silence can be crippling.

Even when you know there is no reason to feel shame and you want to speak out about the problem, it can still be difficult. A newspaper reporter recently asked me why I became involved in my local chapter of the National Alliance on Mental Illness (NAMI). I gave her four reasons: (1) because I am part of a local advisory group to the department of mental health, (2) because I am an advocate for people with autism, whose needs are similar to those with mental illness, (3) because I like to root for the underdog, and (4) because I have a close family member who suffers from clinical depression and anxiety. The fourth response was the most direct reason for my joining and volunteering for NAMI. So why couldn't I just say that in the first place? The answer is stigma.

Why would stigma affect me? After all, I am an advocate and supporter of those who have neurobiological illnesses. I understand the biological nature of these illnesses and know they are no more shameful than having an inadequate production of insulin (as with diabetes) or an excess of cholesterol in the bloodstream. However, I also know my understanding may have little effect on how the public thinks.

Public perception is even more difficult for children and teens to navigate. Kids who struggle with anxiety or depression believe their friends will see them differently if they know about their problems. They fear—as do adults—that they will be seen as deficient, weak, or just different. And when you are a child or teen, being different is like having leprosy. So, even if we disagree with the "silent approach", we need to respect our kid's concerns about disclosure. Stigma rules our actions, even though there is nothing shameful to hide. How crazy is that?

Even my use of the word "crazy" is an example of the subtle way stigma has influenced our society. We use the same term to describe "brain illness" as we do to indicate something is "ridiculous" or "out of control." The loose use of such terms contributes to the public's misunderstanding of neurobiological illnesses.

Public Misperceptions

Why do we still have the problem of stigma in the twenty-first century? One reason is because scientific understanding of the brain is far behind the knowledge of other biological systems. The research is just not as plentiful. For years, study of the brain was delayed because of a general assumption that mental illnesses were either spiritual problems or indicative of sin or immorality in the parents or child. Unfortunately, some religious communities took part in spreading such harmful rumors by attributing much mental suffering to spiritual deficiencies, lack of faith, or even demon possession.

While immorality and spiritual problems certainly afflict people with mental illness—*all* of humanity is stricken with these problems—there is no evidence they are more likely to occur in those with social, emotional, or behavioral challenges. Similarly, character flaws in individuals are present in our population regardless of the presence of neurobiological illness. However, the fact that these attitudes existed has led to an uninformed public and to psychological theories that have spread misconceptions. One of these theories states that social, emotional, or behavioral differences are caused by weaknesses in human character or poor parenting.

In response to these allegations, research increasingly demonstrates there is a biological basis for many social, emotional, and behavioral challenges. In addition, with the exception of severe neglect or abuse (which can trigger a tendency toward neurobiological illness), parents are not to blame for their child's brain disorders anymore than they are to blame for their child's intestinal, heart, or immune system malfunction. Furthermore, while overly permissive or authoritarian parenting can create problems, they rarely cause actual brain impairments or mental illness.

My purpose here is not to give a thorough review of the evidence that proves the biological nature of social, emotional, and behavioral problems. Other resources better address the topic.

I mention this simply to illustrate how lack of knowledge has put unnecessary worry, guilt, and doubt into the minds of people who are already strained by the day-to-day symptoms of these conditions.

One dictionary definition of "stigma" is "a mark of disgrace or discredit."[8] The word "disgrace" means to "degrade from a position of honor." For many individuals with social, emotional, or behavioral challenges, the public's unconscious bias has deprived them of their honor. What we need to clearly understand is that this disgrace has been sorely misplaced! Honor is due to people with neurobiological or psychological illness, as it is to all people. Some of the most courageous and honorable individuals I know live with these chronic conditions. We also need to know that God extends His grace (undeserved favor) to *all* of humanity.

The Harm of Misplaced Disgrace

One of the biggest problems of misplaced disgrace is the shame it produces. Even if the disgrace has no merit, people suffering from neurobiological illnesses often respond to the reactions of others and are motivated to hide the source of their disgrace. Unfortunately, by hiding their difficulties and abiding by the unspoken rule not to disclose the problem, people with these conditions and their families often end up with a host of other issues that further complicate the illness.

I have heard it said that neurobiological conditions are not "casserole" illnesses, which means people are less likely to bring casseroles and get-well cards to the families of those who are ill or hospitalized due to a mental illness. Sometimes the reason for this is because people are concerned but do not know what to say or how to comfort the family. So they just stay away. In some cases, stigma might prevent the family from disclosing that a family member is ill or hospitalized, so others don't know help is needed.

Regardless of the reason, the tendency to be silent and isolate can delay the recovery process for the whole family. There are several reasons for this. First, neurobiological illnesses affect a person's self-esteem more than other conditions, and those affected need affirmation to keep a balanced view of themselves. As with other illnesses, receiving cards and visits from friends and family helps a person realize that he or she is important, loved, and missed in spite of the illness. It also helps the person identify his or her behavior as part of an illness and not as a personal defect. If this positive feedback is not present and the person is left in isolation for too long, he or she is more likely to adopt a negative self-perception. A second concern is that if isolation leads to the individual losing friends and the support of family, he or she is more likely to develop secondary mental illness such as more serious depression or anxiety. This in turn, produces more isolation and a vicious cycle is born.

In addition to isolation, another negative effect of stigma is that it compels people to try to overcome their brain illness with their own "mental toughness" or positive thinking alone, which can prevent them from seeking the medical help they need. National statistics tell us that the average time interval between the onset of symptoms of mental illness and its actual treatment is ten years.[9] Even with serious symptoms, a person may delay seeking treatment to avoid the stigma associated with his or her condition until those symptoms become very damaging to the person and potentially to his or her family.

As with other illnesses, early intervention is the key to controlling more serious manifestations of social, emotional or behavior disorders. In fact, scientific studies reveal that delays in mental health treatment lead to more serious episodes of the illness and brain cell destruction with each episode. Research also shows that untreated mental illness increases the risk of early dementia.[10] Clearly, it is important for people with neurobiological illnesses to seek an evaluation and get treatment as soon as they suspect their behavior may be attributed to more than a temporary phase.

Pride, Shame, and Stigma

What do we do with the personal sense of shame or failure we might feel when a neurobiological illness affects a member of our family? How can we prevent stigma from isolating us and delaying us from getting the help we need? One way is by getting a better understanding of pride and shame. Let's start our discussion with exploring the concept of shame.

There are two main types of shame. The first is the shame that comes about when we are convicted out of our moral compass or a revelation of our misdeeds. This type of "divine" shame is healthy because it leads to repentance and a closer walk with God. For example, we can become aware of sin in our lives, turn from it, and God will use this to draw us closer to Him. The second type of shame comes about when our pride and/or perceived self-sufficiency has been wounded. While this shame can also lead us to godly repentance from our perception of self-sufficiency, Satan tries to take it a step further. He attempts to use the shame to make us self-conscious and embarrassed so we will isolate ourselves from others and hide our perceived weakness. This is the sort of shame we want to avoid.

I want to share with you a story that illustrates both kinds of shame. This example also gives us some insight into the effects of pride, as well. I know of a father and mother whose handsome and successful son had been an honor student and sports star in high school. His parents were very proud of his achievements and reputation. In his junior year, he began to struggle socially, his grades began to drop, and he began to associate with a wild crowd. Later, he was diagnosed with bipolar disorder, which explained the rapid change in his behavior. In the weeks to follow, this family had to admit they had become temporarily ashamed of their son when undiagnosed bipolar stole his good reputation and place in high school society.

Any parent in this situation would feel a similar sense of disappointment and loss. However, this family realized their *intense* feelings of shame may have been an indication of having too much pride in the first place. This kind of shame was temporarily helpful because it helped this family to repent of a pride of which they were not even aware. However, remaining shamed over this situation would not be helpful to anyone involved. The family moved past their shame and is now proud of how their child is learning to manage his serious illness.

You can probably relate to how the parents in this family vacillated between pride and the different kinds of shame. Each of us has experienced similar spontaneous and short-lived bursts of pride and shame. God created our brains so we could experience these emotions, as well as many others. The problem comes when we continue to dwell in either pride or shame and allow it to rule how we live. Neither of these opposing feelings is where God leads us to dwell. Christ came to set us free from living in either camp.

The Bible gives us clear instruction on the problem of pride. Proverbs 16:18 tells us, "Pride goes before destruction, a haughty spirit before a fall." In 2 Samuel 22:28, we read, "You [God] save the humble, but your eyes are on the haughty to bring them . . . low" (brackets added). In biblical terms, "the haughty" refers to those who put faith in their own achievements, as if they created them in their own strength. Prideful people tend to not give heartfelt thanks to God for their blessings. They think they deserve their blessings because of their skill, hard work, family of origin, or status in society. Prideful people might also put faith in the achievements and status of their offspring.

In contrast, humble people know that God grants blessings according to His awesome power and authority and that humans have no right to demand gifts or certain outcomes. They realize that any talent or possessions they have are gifts that could disappear at any moment. They know God's decisions are above their ability to understand (see Job 42:1-3). Humble people learn to be less overwhelmed when trials come, because they realize their vulnerability and dependence on God. Their blessings come from living a life connected to God and from experiencing a bit of heaven on earth.

In Proverbs 16:19, we read that it is "better to be lowly in spirit and among the oppressed than to share plunder with the proud." While shame can discourage us temporarily, the humility we gain from it will be worth far more than the hurt we endure. We may come to this realization more quickly than our children, but as they age and begin to grapple with the reality of their limitations, it is something we can pass on to them. One of our most important jobs as parents is to become spiritually mature so we can offer God's wisdom and comfort to our children when

> One of our most important jobs as parents is to become spiritually mature so we can offer God's wisdom and comfort to our children when they need it.

they need it. In this way, we can help our neurologically challenged children move on, accept their weaknesses, and live victoriously in God's grace.

As parents of children with social, emotional, or behavioral difficulties, we cannot allow attacks against our pride to make us feel unworthy for reasons unrelated to immorality or wrongdoing. We cannot allow the world to make us feel ashamed because our children experience a difficulty that society misunderstands. We cannot allow shame to cause us to shrink away from others and bring about a self-imposed isolation. It is critical that we shed any misplaced disgrace so our children do not subconsciously take it on.

> It is critical that we shed any misplaced disgrace so our children do not subconsciously take it on.

Satan would like nothing better than to use this worldly shame to keep us and our children from doing what God wants us to do with our lives. He would love to make us feel that we are not loved as adopted children of the King. He wants to keep us so consumed with hiding our defects that we fail to get on with the business of doing God's work.

God does not want us to live in shame. He wants us to live in His spirit, which gives us power, love, and self-discipline (see 2 Timothy 1:7). He wants us to be wise in the ways of His kingdom and realize that He makes no mistakes—especially in the creation of His beloved children. Each of us was created with unique physical, spiritual, and intellectual capacities and specific strengths and weaknesses. God gave us both our abilities and disabilities to demonstrate His glory (see John 9:1-3; Romans 12:6-8). Remember, while it is okay to feel temporary shame for immoral behavior, you cannot let Satan's world convince you that the neurobiological differences in your family are shameful.

1. In what ways have you or your family felt embarrassment or shame over your child's challenges?

   _____

   _____

   _____

   _____

2. Were these moments of shame or embarrassment a result of your wounded pride (worldly shame), a result of your child's immoral behavior (godly shame), or a result of both? (You may need to really examine your thoughts to answer this question.)

_____

_____

_____

3. In what ways have you or your child felt stigma (decreased honor) from others as a result of your child's challenges?

_____

_____

_____

4. In what ways have you or your child felt the need to be silent about the challenges you are facing? How is this affecting each of you?

_____

_____

_____

Daily Challenges of Stigma

Once we gain God's perspective on our situation, we can receive an overall sense of spiritual peace. However, we still have to respond each day to the stigma surrounding us. Some people will continue to misunderstand us or may hold our child or family in lower esteem because of the disability. And while the public health educator in me wants to proclaim to the world the facts about neurobiological illness so my family and yours can live without secrets, there are certain restraints that prevent this.

For instance, if God's peace has not yet overruled our child's concern about others' perceptions, making a public announcement may negatively affect him or her. No matter how much we might dislike it, we have to disclose information about our child carefully in order to prevent unnecessary gossip or misunderstandings. The goal is to allow our child to face their condition and its effects at a pace that is comfortable for him or her. Of course, this does not mean we cannot tell anyone about our situation—we just have to share it with people we trust or on a need-to-know-basis. This is a very personal decision that members of your family need to discuss and decide together.

When the Church Inflicts Hurt

I wish I could say all churchgoers are gracious and understanding people who have universally come to the aid of those with social, emotional, or behavioral problems. It is true that some are understanding and supportive, but, as I mentioned previously, other Christians have been not only unhelpful but also hurtful. I have heard stories of families who abandoned their churches and their faith based on the responses they received from Christians to their mental illness or behavior disorders. I have also known people who lived with tremendous neurological suffering for years due to the vocal opinions of churchgoers who believed that taking medication was not a "Christian" thing to do.

In order to make sense of these harmful opinions, we again need to remember that brain science is still in its infancy, and that public opinion reflects years of improper conclusions regarding neurobiological illnesses, their causes, and treatment. In fact, some psychologists who believe brain disorders are caused by improper parenting are still in practice. For years, professionals blamed autism and schizophrenia on parents, even coining terms such as "refrigerator mother" to explain their assumption that autistic behaviors stemmed from the emotional frigidity of the mother. Unfortunately, many Christians subscribed to these theories along with the rest of the population.

Some well-meaning Christians have told individuals with brain disorders that deeper faith and prayer are the answers. One time, when I disclosed to a Christian friend that I was feeling depressed and was going to a doctor for a consultation, she cried out, "Oh, no, you just need Jesus!" This dear friend meant the best for me, and she was right that I desperately need Jesus. However, it turned out that I needed antidepressants as well.

When this friend was having gallbladder attacks, I doubt anyone discouraged her from the surgery and medication the doctor recommended. So why is it sometimes deemed acceptable for one person to seek medical help for a gastrointestinal problem but unacceptable for another to seek medical help for a central nervous system problem? One reason is that people confuse the brain with the spirit, and they conclude that all brain problems are spiritual problems.

Distinguishing the Brain, Mind, and Spirit

In the following proposed model and explanation of the brain, mind, and spirit, I make no claims to having expert knowledge as a theologian or neuroscientist. I do not claim to fully or even marginally understand the function and interaction of the brain, mind, and spirit, and I doubt that humans, in general, will ever be able to completely comprehend them. We are truly fearfully and wonderfully made. Accordingly, my humble explanation is based only on my reasonable knowledge and training in the Scriptures and in health sciences. In spite of these limitations, I hope this overly simplified but commonsense approach will alleviate some confusion in regard to the relationship between the brain, the mind, and the spirit, and their effect on behavior.

The *brain* is the biological structure that houses neurons. These neurons carry electrical signals from one place to another in response to neurochemicals. Brain cells produce these neurochemicals, and they are one of the keys to keeping our brain working in the way we expect. If the structure of these or supporting cells are altered or damaged, if chemicals are inadequately or overly produced, or if electrical communication pathways are slowed or compromised, our brain will not function optimally.

In contrast to the brain, the *mind* is intangible, which means we cannot see it, feel it, or touch it. In ways not understood, our mind takes stored and new information from the brain and spirit to plan, organize, and direct our body (in action and in thought). The physical structure of our brain, neurochemicals, and the presence and activity of communication pathways between brain structures influence brain function. If our brain suffers structural damage, if neurochemicals are in scarce or overabundant supply, or if the pathways of electrical communication are altered, the brain may provide faulty information to our mind. Our mind uses this information (whether faulty or correct) to direct our thoughts and actions accordingly. This is how faulty brain input can lead to unproductive social, emotional, or behavioral responses.

The *spirit*, like the mind, is also intangible, and it is not well understood. What we do know is that after God's physical creation of man, He breathed into him to impart life. It may be that spirit was breathed into him as well, so that men and women would be made in the image of God, who is spirit (see Genesis 1:27; Genesis 2:7; John 4:24). It is the spirit that makes humans unique in God's creation, for they are the only part of God's creation into which He breathed and the only creation He made in His image. It is with our spirit that we understand spiritual things, and it is God's spirit (The Holy Spirit) within us that allows our mind to understand the things of God (see 1 Corinthians 2:14).

So our spirit helps direct our mind by giving spiritual insight and discernment to direct responses. This is how the Holy Spirit within us influences us to make godly decisions. Simultaneously, our brain gives our mind information received from our senses and other environmental input. Information from both spirit and brain is compared to past knowledge and memories. Our mind receives this input and directs our body to act in a number of different ways based on both neural input (from the brain) and spiritual input. This simplified interconnection between the spirit, brain, and mind is depicted in the following illustration:

RELATIONSHIP BETWEEN BRAIN, MIND & SPIRIT

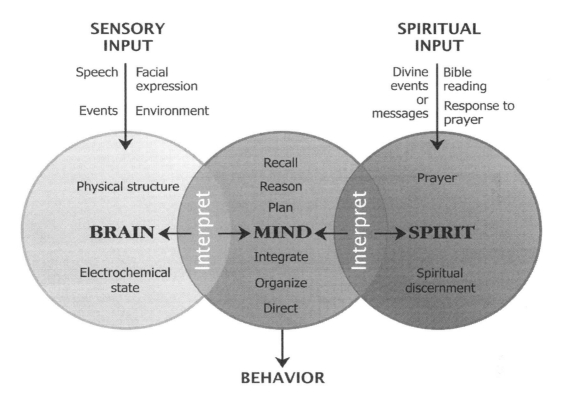

Sensory input is perceived by the *brain*, while spiritual experiences are perceived by the *spirit.* The brain and spirit communicate only *indirectly* through the mind, which interprets and integrates information from both areas. Behavior results from the complex interaction of *all three* entities (i.e. brain, spirit, mind).

Theologians would agree that the biological structure of the brain is not capable of changing spiritual truth. Conversely, most of us do not expect spiritual truth to change the physical structure and function of the brain. The brain responds to input from our senses and emits electrochemical responses, while the spirit responds to input from spiritual forces in ways we do not understand. The mind receives input from both the spirit and the brain and participates in the interpretation of the input. *However, the mind does not have complete control over either the spirit or the brain.*

This limited authority of the mind explains why people can have an intellectual understanding of God but not have the Holy Spirit within them—the Bible tells us that even demons believe in Jesus (see James 2:19). This is also why our spirit can tell us to remain peaceful in all circumstances while our brain is simultaneously directing the production and release of stress hormones. There is a disconnect between spirit and brain that the mind can only *partially* rectify. Therefore, behavior typically results from the complex interaction of spirit, brain, and mind *together*. This is why the *best* interventions for social, emotional, or behavior disorders are usually directed at developing optimal brain function (medication or other neurological therapies), thought or behavior exploration and training (counseling or psychotherapy), and spiritual enrichment (prayer, active belief in a higher power).

Faith and Healing

One might argue that God could override this disconnect between brain and spirit and heal our brains based on the spiritual insights we receive. Of course He can! The manner in which the brain, mind, and spirit *usually* function does not limit God's power in any way—in fact, nothing limits God's power. He is the master healer and the sovereign physician, and He can heal whomever He wants in whatever way He wants. He can alter the structure and function of the brain, heart, kidney, or anything, at His will. We have biblical evidence that sometimes He chooses to work miracles with no medical intervention (see Matthew 9:22), while at other times He seems to work miracles by altering biological processes with the aid of medical techniques (see 2 Kings 20:1-7).

However, it is not the typical way of things for the brain and spirit to work in perfect sync with the mind. If it were, we would always act based on the spirit that dwells within us. In Romans 7:19, the apostle Paul expresses his frustration over this very issue when he says, "For what I do is not the good I want to do; no, the evil I do not want to do—this I keep on doing." Unfortunately, the normal order in our world is for our brain, spirit, and mind to be disconnected. Just as we do not expect to see people defy God's law of gravity and fly into space on any given day, we should not expect to see the brain and spirit acting in complete accord with one another. This is why we cannot blame neurological disorders that cause social, emotional, and behavioral problems solely on a lack of faith or spirituality.

Of course, faith *is* important to the healing of brain disorders and the improvement of social, emotional, and behavioral challenges. Believers are instructed to pray and have faith that God can and will work miracles at His discretion for all sorts of illnesses. In this way, faith is as important to healing brain problems as it is to healing gastrointestinal or kidney disorders. However, because many people confuse the brain with the spirit, they think spiritual enlightenment *alone* will physically heal the brain. Ironically, these same people would not expect spiritual enlightenment alone to heal the heart or liver.

So how do we handle the reality that those suffering from brain illnesses are sometimes discouraged from getting medical help? The brain is as much a part of the physical body as any other organ, so this sort of attitude is unreasonable and unfair, but it exists. The best way I know to change this view is to educate people to the degree needed so they understand the biological nature of brain illnesses and the separation of the brain, mind, and spirit. This process is often not practical, and progress will be slow, but it is in the interest of our children and their children to keep working to educate the public.

5. Based on this discussion, how do the brain, spirit, and mind affect behavior?

    _____

    _____

    _____

6. Why is it not correct, under normal circumstances (without special divine intervention), to attribute the cause of behavior to spiritual influences alone?

    _____

    _____

    _____

Personal and Community Destigmatization

As you may have experienced, the public's understanding of social, emotional, and behavioral disorders is clearly lacking. While there have been some improvements within the last decade, there is still much to be done. It would be nice if enlightened professionals in the field could take care of educating the public so we could raise our children in an environment of empathy, understanding, and support. However, the truth is that the biggest changes often come from grassroots efforts within the affected community.

A number of years ago, I attended a conference in which the speaker asked the audience who the movers and shakers were when it came to issues related to autism. As the mom of a child with these problems, I looked around the room eagerly, hoping to learn the name and contact information of a professional (or professionals) who could help me. However, the overwhelming response was that it was the *parents* of children with autism who were the strongest agents of positive change. In that moment, the reality of my situation became clear.

It was *my calling* to cause change and improvement in the system of autism care, not to look for some professional to have the answers to my problems. Among other things, this revelation motivated me to found SLATE, which, as I mentioned, now serves more than 100 children each year.

My work as a parent promoting systemic improvement is not unusual. Historically, parents looking out for the interests of their children have been the initiators of many—if not most—of our systems of public service. They are often the best equipped to affect positive change because they have intimate knowledge of the problems and live with them every day. While each of us might not be called to found an organization, we all have a role in making the world a better place for children and adults with these types of disorders. Because we deal with all different sorts of symptoms and diagnoses in our children, we are among the most knowledgeable and motivated to lead the cause of destigmatizing social, emotional, and behavioral disorders.

But how can we personally initiate change? Perhaps the best way is to simply share our story. This is easier to do if our child has problem behavior in full view of others—in which case it can actually be a *relief* to disclose the root cause of the behavior. It can be more difficult to disclose our stories if the condition is subtle and easier to hide. In such instances, we might go years before anyone detects a particular illness. Of course, this runs the risk that people will come to their own conclusions about why our child behaves or socializes in a certain way. They may guess something is worse than it really is or conclude that we, the parents, are the problem. However, if we tell our story, we open the possibility that people will grow to be compassionate and helpful—even if their initial response is not ideal.

Breaking the Silence

As difficult as it might be, breaking the silence over social, emotional, or behavioral disorders is the best way to reduce stigma. For this reason, it is important to talk to people you trust in your own time. When people learn that an average family like yours is struggling with one of these problems, they begin to realize it can happen within *any* family. If you are comfortable talking about the problem, others will gain comfort in talking about it as well. This changes society little by little and opens up the possibility that one day it will be easier for your children to talk about the issues and more comfortable for their peers to listen.

If your child requests that you be cautious in disclosing information, you need to honor that request until he or she feels differently. In this case, you might want to participate in an organization that has a goal of reducing stigma, such as the National Alliance on Mental Illness (NAMI). This organization has a campaign to reduce stigma, and it actually offers training to persons with mental illness so they can learn to tell their stories. Even if your child or another family member is not ready to share, he or she will gain support, acceptance, and strength by associating with such groups. NAMI and other organizations also have public events that break the silence of these issues and make people aware of illnesses not freely discussed in daily life. Of course, the power of these groups to effect change in our communities depends on their volunteers, so it is important to get involved to the fullest extent possible.

Finally, be sure to combat stigma by saying a kind word to other families who might be struggling with neurobiological disorders. For example, if you see a child exhibiting poor behavior in a grocery store and you suspect a neurobiological disorder to be the cause, take a moment to sympathize with the family or offer to hold their place in line if they must chase down a child. Sending a card to someone who is struggling with depression is another powerful way to break down a wall of silence that he or she may have inadvertently built.

7. To what degree are you or your loved ones living in a state of isolation from others who could be of help or support?

_____

_____

_____

_____

8. Who could you invite to be an ally to support you and your child?

_____

_____

_____

9. In what ways can you contribute to reducing stigma against persons with social, emotional, or behavioral disorders?

_____

_____

_____

_____

God's Perspective

Finally, as we struggle with what the world might think of us and our family, it is critical to immerse ourselves in what God thinks. Thankfully, the Bible is clear that God extends grace to the afflicted. Through Jesus' example, we know He has compassion on those who have been afflicted with a variety of illnesses, for He personally touched individuals who were afflicted by demons, who were blind and lame, or who had leprosy—the most stigmatized illness of the era. God has also clearly stated that He does not necessarily inflict illness upon people as a result of a personal sin, as the stories of Job and the man born blind reveal (see Job 1:8; John 9:1-3). The One who really matters does not hold any stigma against neurobiological issues. He has nothing but compassion and an offer of grace to those who follow Him. As a matter of fact, He is proud of us with a godly pride. As Isaiah 62:5 states, "As a bridegroom rejoices over his bride, so will your God rejoice over you." Let's live with this reality ruling our hearts.

> As we struggle with what the world might think of us and our family, it is critical to immerse ourselves in what God thinks.

10. Review on paper *and out loud* what God thinks about your family and your child. Post His written word and speak His thoughts frequently throughout each day.

_____

_____

_____

Prayer Thought

Lord, please help me as I struggle to overcome feelings of needless shame that the world has put upon me or my child. Help me to feel the power and love that You give and to speak out against stigma and silence in a way that honors my family. Give me wisdom to treat others with the esteem You have given to me. Thank You for Your grace to all. Amen.

Chapter 6

ATTITUDE CHECK: THE POWER OF PARENTS LIVING THE TRUTH

It was a beautiful winter day, and I was taking a walk to the mailbox. As soon as I saw what was in the box, however, I let out a weary sigh. As I pulled out the mail and began walking toward the house, I was already thinking about how I would feel when I opened one particular envelope I had seen. I began to dread it. I walked slowly, putting it off for as long as possible. No, it wasn't a bill, a foreclosure notice, or a letter from an estranged friend or family member. It was a Christmas card—one that possibly contained a letter and family photo. Dread of all dreads. How would this one leave me feeling? Most likely with mixed emotions. I was glad to hear from loved ones, but sad as well.

As much as I truly cared about my family and friends and wanted to stay in touch, sometimes the success stories I read in these letters grieved me. While this was certainly not the sender's intended purpose for "the season," I still felt this way. I remember that one year almost every letter brought me to tears because the family updates seemed so normal and rewarding, while we had experienced a tough year.

Then there were the lovely family photos—those perfect-looking parents and children all smiling at the camera. I was lucky if I could get all of my family members to smile in the general direction of the camera. This is not to say I wasn't proud of them because I was. But my story did not represent the "American dream"—equal opportunity and overcoming all challenges with hard work. My family was precious, but we did not have the usual ups and downs; we had more serious issues. I hadn't bargained for being a mom to this group. Parenting seemed *much too difficult.* Although I tried to will myself to feel good about my situation, sometimes it was hard. How could I parent well and feel content with my lot?

Responding to the Challenges

Not long after this difficult winter, I came across an interesting statement in a newspaper article. The article reviewed a book written to help married couples continue to communicate and get along once children are born into the family. The focus of the book seemed to be about how children forever change their parent's lives and how to keep marriages strong within that reality. The newspaper reporter interviewed one of the authors of the book (Stacie Cockrell), who made a statement about surrendering yourself to a new life when children come along. She said, "Children are never the problem. The problem is how we grown-ups respond to the challenge of parenting."[11] It is important to realize that neither this author nor her book were making commentary on special-needs parenting—she was talking about problems in marriage. However, I couldn't help but wonder about the truth of this statement for parents, especially as it relates to *special-needs parenting in particular.*

My first thought about this statement was to clarify that while I agree that children are not necessarily "the problem," it would be false to say that children are all born alike, equal, or with a "blank slate." For a variety of reasons, some are definitely more difficult to parent than others, and also put more of a strain on a marriage. I am not just saying this because I have found parenting to be difficult. All of us probably know some mom or dad who has confessed to evaluating herself/himself as a wonderful parent until the "difficult child" came along. However, I also must agree that the way grown-ups respond to parenting challenges is also key—we are called to parent well no matter what.

Again, we must be reminded that Cockrell's statement was not made with special needs families in mind, nor about the relative ease of parenting different children. However, I must say I generally agree with her overriding commentary about children not being the problem. I also admit it can seem unfair. I certainly gave 100% effort toward parenting, but I was not getting the affirmation and success it seemed I deserved. It looked easy for other people. Yes, I had children who were more than a little challenging, but couldn't I rise above and feel as if I had excelled in parenting the way I had excelled at other things in my life? I really wanted to get the kind of positive feedback I would expect to get from a boss in the workplace or from a professor in college.

Of course, receiving feedback as a parent does not happen this way. We do not get report cards in Parenting 101. We cannot earn an A with extra credit, and we cannot be assured that our work will earn us promotions or the outcome we want—even if we do everything we think we are supposed to do. We can read books and try different techniques, but no one parenting approach will solve all the challenges of our specific child—especially those techniques designed for typical children. It often seems we just have to do our best and hope to enjoy it along the way. To some degree this is true, but I wanted guidelines to give me some confidence and comfort.

Five Principles for Effective and Enjoyable Parenting

For most of us, parenting takes up a significant portion of our lives, and it would certainly seem there should be some principles out there to help us be effective and enjoy the process, even with special-needs kids. We know that God expects us to correct our children (see Proverbs 22:6,15; 29:15,17), and we know that we are to raise our children in the training and instruction of the Lord (see Ephesians 6:4). How we live out these scriptures in real life is another matter. However, it is not my intent to translate these verses into practical application in this book, as other sources do this in great detail.

In this chapter, I want to explore some ways to better understand parenting children with special needs so we can be effective *and enjoy the process*. I believe God intends each of us to benefit from parenting our children, even if it is difficult and painful at times. I will begin by outlining five truths I learned during my search to find keys to successful and enjoyable parenting. Living in the light of these truths helped me regain my confidence, parent well, and have some fun doing it. I pray they will help you as well. These five principles are:

Principle #1   Even difficult children are a blessing from the Lord.

Principle #2   Expectations and "childing" will affect a parent's attitude.

Principle #3   Accepting God's truths will lead to effective and enjoyable parenting.

Principle #4   The elements of success for work and school are different than those for parenting.

Principle #5   Perseverance in parenting is priceless.

We will examine each of these principles in turn.

Principle #1: Even Difficult Children Are a Blessing from the Lord

In Psalm 127:3, we read that children "are a reward" from the Lord. During my years of parenting, I cannot honestly say that I always agreed with this statement. On some days I could see the deep blessings my children bestowed on me —but on other days, not so much. Even though I trusted the truth of this verse, I often *felt* as if my children were "a worry" from the Lord rather than a reward. They gave my life great meaning and joy, but they also left me feeling clueless, weak, and insecure. I think many parents whose children have social, emotional, or behavioral difficulties feel the same way.

A Reality Check

One day as I was pondering the duality of the situation, it dawned on me why even difficult children are a blessing. It is not because they adore us and always make us proud, or because they look good in the eyes of the world. Instead, it is because these children give us a reality check about who we are in relation to God, our Father. The truth we often forget or ignore is that when compared to God, we really *are* clueless, weak, and insecure, and difficult children are good at reminding us of this vulnerability. They help us recognize we do not control our lives as much as we would like to think. Additionally, they teach us that while education, financial security, good looks, and talent are helpful in life, they do not bring us lasting peace when bad things happen. In short, difficult children remind us how much we need God.

> Difficult children remind us how much we need God.

Children really *are* a reward and a blessing, but not always in the way we would like or expect. Rather, they are a blessing because (1) they cause us to face the truth about ourselves, and (2) they create a lot of work, which gives us opportunities to mature and persevere in our walk with God. Are you smiling yet? It's true. Children are character builders—and godly character leads to significant blessing in our lives. Through our difficult children, we are admitted into the School of Hard Knocks. As it turns out, this is a great blessing if God is our headmaster.

It is important to note that our children cannot *force* us to persevere and develop godly character. Certainly, there are many parents who have given up or done wrong in spite of the opportunity to raise their children well. Regardless of the situation, we still choose *how* we will respond to the stressors in our lives—and parenting kids with social, emotional, and behavioral problems can cause some significant stressors. However, if we choose well, parenting our children will provide us with an unmatched opportunity to work, think, soul search, grow, learn, and live in a much deeper and more meaningful way. Mythologist and author Joseph Campbell summed it up well when he said, "Great opportunities are missed by many because they come disguised as hard work." As we parent, we need to continually remind ourselves that the hard work of each day presents opportunities for us to become better or bitter. Our responses have the power to greatly influence the quality of our life and the example we leave for our children.

The Blessing of Hard Work

Even though we rarely love hard work as we are doing it, the blessing is that we often receive significant gain after the work is done. For example, we might not enjoy the hard work of painting a room in our home or struggling to earn a college degree, but when the project is finished, we will receive great satisfaction from the results. Knowing we have done our best with our challenging children will give us the same satisfaction, and it will present us with the opportunity to become more Christlike. As we encounter difficult situations and cry out to God for help, He helps us through the struggle, and we deepen our trust in Him and build godly character.

In his book *Sacred Parenting*, Gary Thomas notes that children shape not only our character but also our very souls. They push us to get in touch with our spiritual selves. Even if our children do not "turn out perfectly," we can receive blessings from the *process*. We are blessed by seeing the similarities between our parenting experiences and how God loves us when *we* are difficult, and we can learn to show that same love to others. In short, we can become more holy.[12]

Most of us do not view difficult parenting experiences this way, especially in the beginning. We see them as traumatic disruptions to our status quo—and, to be truthful, they are. However, in spite of the pain we endure in parenting children with special needs, it can also be joyful! Some of the intense hurdles we face will be followed by equally dramatic solutions. Trials do end—or at least change in intensity—and because the lows may be frequent, we really learn to appreciate the mountaintop moments. Even during crises, we can learn to celebrate small moments of progress and find humor in the situation. This ability to celebrate and see humor in the midst of difficulties is a huge blessing in and of itself.

Our attitude plays a big part in whether we experience more pain or more joy in parenting. The choice we have to make is whether we will say "yes" to our opportunity to grow in grace as we parent our child, or whether we will choose to shrink back in fear and hopelessness.

1. In what ways can you see that your difficult child has been a blessing?

_____

_____

_____

Principle #2: Expectations and "Childing" Will Affect a Parent's Attitude

When we say "yes" to our parenting opportunity, we choose to view the challenge as a means of growth. Keeping this attitude in the midst of daily trials is difficult, but we will have greater success if we analyze our parenting expectations and recognize how much "childing" influences our view of how effective we are being as parents. We will examine each of these points in turn.

Expectations and Attitude

According to Hugh F. Johnston, MD, each of us enters into parenthood with a certain set of expectations. These expectations are influenced by our childhood experiences, what we have seen in other families, and by our age, education, and personality, among other factors. Even the sort of kids we used to be and the way in which we were parented will play a part in developing our expectations. For instance, if we were compliant as children and rarely needed strong discipline, we tend to assume our kids will be the same. We will expect to have a peaceful and orderly home. On the other hand, if we were monsters as children but our parents did a good job reining us in, we will expect our children to learn better behavior over time. Every situation we faced has influenced the skills and tricks we have picked up along the way.[13]

Unfortunately, these expectations will not necessarily be met by our children with social, emotional, or behavioral problems. They may move more quickly to anger than we did as a child, or they may be weepy, clingy, and insecure. They may be all over the place all the time, practically climbing the walls as they leave a trail of havoc in their wake. They may spit at us or throw hour-long tantrums. Or alternatively, they may spend recess time reading in the classroom while the other children play dodgeball.

If we were popular and easygoing as children, the spitting and tantrums are really going to throw us for a loop! We will likely be shocked and embarrassed at our child's behavior and at a loss as to how to respond. Parenting will seem very difficult for us, as we have no prior experience with this sort of behavior. On the other hand, if we were difficult as a child but had a parent who could handle it, we might feel in control as we use the same techniques our parents used successfully with us. Or we might feel angry, fearful, and confused because our parents never did know how to settle us, and this child brings back memories of being out of control.

Hopefully, these examples demonstrate how our family experiences pre-condition us for parenting. This is why some behaviors will be easier for us to handle than others and why some parts of parenting will seem too hard. Just having this knowledge will be helpful, so it is important to keep our attitude up! Parenting challenges are just part of the growing process, and we will learn and adjust to our particular situation over time.

2. What sort of child were you growing up? How does that relate to your expectations in parenting your child?

_____

_____

_____

"Childing" and Attitude

In addition to our expectations, the relationship we have with our children will also affect our ability to adjust and respond to certain parenting situations. Dr. Johnston describes this relationship as "parenting and childing." While we all know the definition of parenting, fewer of us are familiar with the concept of "childing."

"Parenting," of course, is what we do for our children. Good parenting means protecting our children from harm and helping them meet their physical, spiritual, and emotional needs. It involves loving our children unconditionally, giving them affection, and teaching them knowledge and skills. "Childing," on the other hand, is what our children do for us as parents. For example, if our children do their day-to-day chores with a reasonably good attitude or show appropriate affection and gratitude to us, we would say they are exhibiting good childing. However, if they are spitting or throwing tantrums, we would say they are exhibiting poor childing.

Poor childing is caused by a variety of sources. Often it comes from a brain disorder as a result of a genetic predisposition, an injury or toxin, or an abnormal developmental environment. While the child is rarely at fault for poor childing, the result is that his or her ability to bond and/or learn from reward and punishment systems is impaired. Dr. Johnston states that what parents often fail to recognize is how much childing affects how they appraise their parenting adequacy. In particular, parents tend to underestimate how profoundly poor childing leads to their misplaced guilt, feelings of incompetence, and, sometimes, correspondingly poor parenting. And poor childing tends to make moms and dads feel ineffective, even if their parenting is good.

3. In what ways do you think your child's "childing" affects your feelings of effectiveness and your parenting?

    _____

    _____

    _____

Let me be clear that the purpose of this discussion is not to blame our children for poor childing so we, the parents, can feel better and justify poor parenting. Rather, the purpose is to acknowledge the truth that some children come into the world with dispositions that can simply be more difficult to parent. Babies are not born with equal temperaments and equal abilities to learn. Realizing this, we need to shed our guilt and feelings of incompetence in raising our difficult children so we can get on with the business of doing the best job possible.

Again, the purpose of this discourse is not to blame our children. Rather, it is to highlight the need for good parenting even in the face of bad childing. While it is helpful to realize that bad childing is present, we have to move forward and be good parents anyway. This is where the rubber meets the road—where the battle is won or lost. It determines whether we will look back at our parenting days with regret or with contentment.

4. How can you parent well in spite of poor childing? (Note: this often requires outside help and support.)

_____

_____

_____

Principle #3: Accepting God's Truths Will Lead to Effective and Enjoyable Parenting

In addition to our expectations as parents and our relationship with our child, our belief system will also play an important part in how effective we are as parents and how much we enjoy the process. What we believe determines how we think, which determines how we behave, which determines much of our future. If we start believing lies, we will set ourselves on an unintended path toward grief and destruction.

I strongly believe that accepting and living God's truths affects our ability to adjust to situations that arise and enjoy the parenting process. However, because we are bombarded each day by the values and beliefs of our society, it is easy for us to unconsciously begin to follow worldly values. In order to live in God's truth, we need to be constantly reminded of what God says and how it differs from worldly lies. There is no substitute for daily Bible reading, prayer, and discussion/support with like-minded people to keep us walking in the truth of God. The following chart can also be helpful in seeing the differences between the truth and the lies.

Lies of the World	Truths of God
We need to practice self-gratification.	We need to practice self-denial (Matthew 16:23-25; Mark 8:34; Luke 9:23).
We need to make a "success" of ourselves and our children.	God expects us to "act justly and to love mercy and to walk humbly with [our] God" (Micah 6:8, brackets added).
We need to promote ourselves.	Our purpose is to promote God (see Ephesians 2:10; 1 Corinthians 10:31).
Joy comes from achieving worldly success.	Joy comes from knowing and understanding God (see Nehemiah 8:10-12; Habakkuk 3:16-18).

We should feel happy all the time. Suffering is abnormal, undesirable, and bad.	Suffering has a purpose—it produces hope, character, and godly obedience (see Romans 5:3-4).
We deserve immediate, fair, and adequate compensation for our pain and suffering.	We will receive more than adequate compensation in God's way and time (see 1 Corinthians 2:9).

The Truth Behind Success and Self-Promotion

Although the benefits of focusing on God's truths and rejecting Satan's lies seem clear in this chart, in real life it can be difficult to consistently follow this course. Our society does a good job in socializing us and rewarding us for believing and living out the lies. We become conditioned by the ridiculous and unhealthy values of the world because they bombard us each and every day.

According to the world's view, achieving success and happiness means receiving money, prestige, or fame. Our society lauds product or self-promotion as a means toward this end. For example, my husband recently read that the Nike Shoe Company has paid Michael Jordan over a billion dollars over the last several years to use his name on the Air Jordan shoe. There is no doubt that Michael Jordan was a great basketball player, but I doubt that he or his basketball shoes have transformed many of our lives. However, our society rewards people for becoming well-known. When success comes into our minds, we must remind ourselves that the world values many things that have limited value or meaning.

Of course, achievement on earth is not inherently evil; however, it can cause problems with our thinking and expectations. For instance, we can become so accustomed to public commendation that we turn into "approval junkies." We become addicted to approval without even realizing it—until the rewards come less frequently. As most of us realize, parenting children with special needs does not come with lots of approval and commendation; in fact, it often comes with sacrificing public status and gaining hard work in its place. This can be a shocking reality if we are used to achievement and the accolades it brings.

Of course, in God's estimation, status reduction is not really a problem. He tells us that our purpose is not to seek personal approval and self-promotion but to do good works and make *Him* famous in the process. In Ephesians 2:10, Paul says, "We are God's workmanship, created in Christ Jesus to do good works." In 1 Corinthians 10:31, he adds, "Whatever you do, do it all *for the glory of God*" (emphasis added). God rewards vastly different behavior than the world does. He hands out accolades for self-denial and humility. Jesus tells us that "he who is least among you all—he is the greatest" (Luke 9:48) and that "if anyone would come after me, he

> God rewards vastly different behavior than the world does.

must deny himself, take up his cross and follow me" (Matthew 16:24). These are radical ways to live in contrast to our culture.

The Truth Behind Busyness and Activity

In our society, busyness is strongly associated with success. Our culture pressures parents to push their children to do many activities so they do not get "left behind." The busier they are, the more they are regarded as capable. As you know, having social, emotional, or behavioral difficulties often interferes with schoolwork, social development, and other skills. This means that during the more challenging periods of their lives our kids may not have full social or occupational schedules. This usually concerns parents, but should it?

There is not an easy answer to this question. In the Western world, children and adults are expected to be busy and productive. In the Bible, we are warned in Ecclesiastes 10:18 and 11:6 not to be idle. From this we can infer that we should encourage our children to keep busy in the activities they are able to do. However, we should guard against feeling guilty and/or worried if they cannot keep up the same pace as the neighbors. Life does not have to be the competition we so often make it.

> In place of constant activity, God would prefer us to teach our children simple yet profound truths.

In place of constant activity, God would prefer us to teach our children simple yet profound truths. Micah 6:8 tells us that the Lord requires us to "act justly and to love mercy and to walk humbly with [our] God" (brackets added). When I feel as if I am falling short in my duties as a person or a parent, it helps to reflect on this verse. These words tell me that I need to prioritize opportunities to teach my children compassion, to do what is right, and to have a relationship with God. It also reminds me to meditate often on God's Word so my thinking becomes more like God's.

God's approach to success is superior to the world's in at least two respects: (1) it frees our children to be who God created them to be instead of striving for the fickle definition of worldly success; (2) we live more joyfully when we concentrate on making God famous instead of ourselves. This freedom and joy are ours if we keep our focus vertical (toward God) instead of horizontal (toward the world).

The Truth Behind Pain and Joy

Not only does the world tell us lies about success, but it also tells us lies about the nature of suffering. Now, let me be clear that I do not mean to minimize the problem and experience of pain. I dislike it as much as anyone, and I work hard to avoid it and help others avoid it as well. God expects us to comfort others in pain, and reducing the emotional and spiritual pain of others is the main reason why I wrote this book. The books of Proverbs and Ecclesiastes also were written to help people become wise so they could avoid the pain that foolishness brings.

The problem is that our society attempts to teach us that we should avoid pain at all costs, look for immediate relief of suffering, and make others pay for the uncomfortable feelings and inconvenience that suffering can bring. From an early age, society teaches us to look for self-gratification and to get it quickly. In addition, Satan tries to make us believe we should feel happy all the time—that suffering is bad and abnormal.

The truth is that while God did not choose suffering for us, it is an important learning tool. I admit this truth is not an easy one to accept. However, as Paul clearly states in Romans 5:3-4, "Suffering produces perseverance; perseverance, character; and character, hope." James also states that we are to "consider it pure joy" when we face trials of many kinds, because we know the testing of our faith develops perseverance (James 1:2-3). We need to remember that even Jesus "learned obedience from what he suffered" (Hebrews 5:8). Suffering is horrible, but it has valuable endpoints—such as hope and obedience—that bring tremendous *eternal* blessing.

Furthermore, we are reminded that the compensation we will receive for our faithfulness to God, even through suffering, will be great. We are promised "new heavens and a new earth," a place where the "sound of weeping and of crying will be heard … no more" (Isaiah 65:17, 19). The sufferings we endure in the present time will seem insignificant when compared to this eternal place. We are promised that our grief will not last forever and that there will be a time when our joy is complete (see John 16:21-24).

In the meantime, of course, we all want to feel some joy in the present. God wants this for us as well. However, instead of temporary blessings such as health, wealth, success, and prestige that the world says we must have to be joyful, God wants us to have the lasting joy that comes from knowing Him and understanding His truths. In Nehemiah 8:12, we read that the people became joyful because "they now understood the words [in Scripture] that had been made known to them" (brackets added). In the same way, we can be joyful even if things in life are not going our way (see Habakkuk 3:16-18).

Recently, my seventeen-year-old shared that in spite of her health problems, she realizes they have no long-term significance for her because of God's presence in her life. The expression of joy on her face when she told me this was indescribable. She was radiant in an other-worldly sort of way. I can think of no better blessing in her life than for her to understand this truth and joy at such a young age. I also suspect she would not have this spiritual insight and peace had she not gone through times of suffering.

The Blessings of Raising a Difficult Child

As we comprehend the difference between the lies of the world and the truths of God, we are able to more easily see the spiritual blessings of raising a difficult or disabled child. Although there are many directions we could go in this discussion, for purposes of this chapter, I will summarize three overarching spiritual blessings.

First, *raising a difficult child makes it easier for us to accept God's truths.* We tend to see the world's lies more clearly when someone we love has difficulty living up to its expectations, and we tend to walk more humbly with God when worldly success does not tempt us to become arrogant. In Matthew 19:23, Jesus states that "it is hard for a rich man to enter the kingdom of heaven." In addition to money, I believe the "riches" He refers to in this passage include talent, popularity, and other gifts. Although some people can handle riches and remain humble, many become arrogant and reduce their felt need for God. In contrast, children with social, emotional, and behavioral problems continually reveal to us how desperately we need supernatural help.

A second blessing of raising a difficult child is that it *helps us develop wisdom, patience, self-control, and gentleness.* These traits are byproducts of the suffering and self-denial that is inherent in parenting a child with special needs. Of course, it is possible to forgo the self-denial and not acquire these wonderful qualities—we can be selfish in any situation if we try hard enough. However, our love for our children usually pushes us into self-denial and, over time, God adds these gifts to our personality. (We will discuss self-denial in greater detail in chapter 7.)

A third blessing of raising a difficult child is that it *deepens our experiences of peace and joy.* If we learn to accept God's truths (blessing #1) and gain wisdom, patience, gentleness, and self-control (blessing #2), we usually have done the work necessary to earn blessing #3—a deeper sense of peace and joy. Peace and joy are the result of *believing* what God says and *acting* on these beliefs. If we really trust God, we will follow His wisdom and do what He says. In His Word, God says that He "will keep in perfect peace him whose mind is steadfast, because he trusts in [Him]" (Isaiah 26:3, brackets added). He also says that if we learn to trust and obey Him, our peace will be "like a river" (Isaiah 48:18).

> Peace and joy are the result of *believing* what God says and *acting* on these beliefs.

To me, this last verse about peace conjures an image of a slow-moving river that winds its way leisurely through the countryside. However, a river can also be turbulent and dangerous. In fact, much like life, most rivers contain both peaceful and turbulent areas. This diversity of river flow suggests that Isaiah may have been referring to some other quality of a river that produces peace. One thought is that rivers are known to produce great growth in the plants along their shores. Ancient civilizations often formed near rivers because they supplied water and food. For farmers, there was and is still an advantage in planting near a river as the crops will have a reliable supply of life-sustaining water.

Our family knows this firsthand, as we own property along the Sacramento River in northern California. One day as we were perusing the area with a landscaper, he expressed amazement at the size and health of the trees that grew on the property. He said they were twice the size of trees in comparable areas with no river nearby. In the same way, when we are steadily fed by God's nourishment, we grow strong and healthy. Peace follows because we do not have to worry about how we will survive and sustain our lives. Although we will experience seasons of turbulence and of rest, we can have peace in His provision.

Do you now see the potential blessings in believing and living God's truth, especially as it relates to our parenting? If we want to live and walk in the truth, we need to keep our focus on the truth. We need to be in God's Word consistently so we regularly renew our minds with His truths as we live our lives and parent our children. Popular culture is constantly in our face and spreading its lies, so we have to intentionally focus on Jesus' culture to think and act as God desires.

5. What lies of the world have led you to be discouraged about your child's situation?

_____

_____

_____

6. What are God's corresponding truths that you will now focus on instead?

_____

_____

_____

_____

Principle #4: The Elements of Success for Work and School are Different than Those for Parenting

It is easy to underestimate the influence the culture around us has on our attitudes toward parenting and child development. Sociologists call this influence the "macrosystem" surrounding a child or family. This is basically just a fancy word to describe how cultures value different ideas about how a person should spend time, gain information, and relate interpersonally. Understanding the basics of our macrosystems will help us see their influence on our lives more clearly.

Edward T. Hall, a cultural anthropologist, classified macrosystems as being either "high context" or "low context."[14] In the United States, the most dominant macrosystem is a low-context culture that tends to come from the Euro-American, urban middle class. It values progress, competition, efficient use of time, and achievement. High-context systems, which are seen in more rural areas and in Native American, Latino American, and some Asian American traditions, tend to emphasize cooperation, tradition, and building character and relationships through human interaction. Note that neither macrosystem is necessarily superior to the other; each system just prepares its members differently for life's challenges.

The type of macrosystem in which we are raised will affect our approach to parenting. If we were raised in a family or culture that was primarily low context, we may find parenting to be more difficult than in high-context cultures, where many skills for parenting are emphasized to a greater degree. Certainly, high-context values such as cooperation, tradition, and building character through relationships relate better to parenting young children than the low-context values of progress, competition, efficiency, and achievement. Infants or special-needs toddlers are not motivated by efficiency or achievement, so moms and dads raised to value these attributes are likely to be frustrated by special-needs parenting, especially in the early years.

The following chart summarizes the values and skills for success we may have learned in our low-context culture as opposed to high-context values and skills that are more helpful in parenting—in particular, special-needs parenting. (Please note that the column headings in this chart were created by me in order to summarize the information described in this chapter. However, the contents of the chart are originally the work of an unidentified author from an unknown source.)

Values and Skills Promoting Work Success (Low Context)	Values and Skills Promoting Parental Adjustment (High Context)
Constantly strive for perfection	Tolerate repeated errors
Make time to pursue independent goals	Make time for family activities
Keep a goal-oriented attitude toward projects	Keep an attitude that reflects the child as the priority

Commit to oneself and one's goals	Commit to one's child and his or her goals
Be efficient	Tolerate chaos and uncertainty
Believe that success is the first priority	Believe that failure produces growth
Focus on the essentials	Digress at times to "smell the roses"
Maintain one's image	Relax and accept embarrassment
Create family life to support a career	Accept that children have their own agenda
Seek concise information	Listen patiently to childish talk
Insist on high standards	Tolerate the lack of certain abilities
Strive to become successful	Strive to become godly
Value the visible, here-and-now life	Value the unseen, eternal life

Hopefully, this chart clarifies, for those of us raised in low-context cultures, why the task of parenting a challenging child can sometimes seem more frustrating than joyful. This can be especially problematic near the beginning of our journey, before we have had time to adjust our expectations, shift our values, and develop new skills. Of course, parenting children with special needs is challenging for parents raised in high-context cultures as well, though the challenges may be seen differently.

While it will be difficult at first for us to modify our focus and develop skills that will be helpful in parenting special-needs children, over time we *will* learn to adjust, and we will find it easier to do so. The more quickly we adjust to this process and develop new attitudes and skills, the easier it will be for us to find joy in parenting our children. For example, the more quickly we learn to tolerate chaos, failure, and uncertainty, the easier it will be for us to begin finding joy in parenting our child with challenges. Taking time to "smell the roses" is also good for our hearts and our souls.

While we have focused on the importance of developing some high-context skills, note that some low-context skills are also beneficial to our children. Valuing achievement and progress can push us to teach our children effectively and to defer instant gratification. We are also more likely to have high expectations for our children if we have learned to value the skills for success in the work world. These skills will be helpful as long as we know how to temper our expectations with the reality of our child's challenges. We should also remember that God is more than capable of using either framework and teaching us the new skills we need.

The last two rows in the right-hand column of the chart contain the most important values for Christians to develop: striving to become godly and valuing the unseen, eternal life. Although none of us has ultimate control over who our children will become as adults, we can always prioritize our personal love toward God and raise our children with this value. And as we learn to value eternal life and teach our children to do the same, it will fuel our joy as well.

Jesus confirmed the importance of these values in Matthew 22:37-38 when He proclaimed that loving God with all our heart, mind, and soul is the greatest commandment and our most important task on earth. We also know that Jesus' (and, thus, God's) desire is to bring us the joy available from living in fellowship with Him (see John 17:13). What a wonderful truth! When we live by these priorities, we will find that we have a better attitude and that parenting a difficult child is a little easier.

7. What values and skills do you need to focus on to maintain a better attitude about parenting your child?

_____

_____

_____

Principle #5: Perseverance in Parenting is Priceless

The fifth and final principle is easy to describe but much more difficult to live by. But, oh, the joys it will bring if we persevere in good parenting!

One of the reasons perseverance is so important in raising our children is because they are watching us and being influenced by us, even when it seems they are not paying attention. Even though the outside world increasingly influences our children as they grow, we are still the most influential people in their lives and the most important ambassadors from God to them. We are designed to be their protector, teacher, coach, and fan. We are the ones who introduce our kids to how joyful life can be if our minds are conformed to Christ. In this, we lay the foundation of hope our children may carry with them through life.

I like how Oswald Chambers described this phenomenon. He said that until others learn to draw on the life of Jesus directly for spiritual nourishment, they will have to draw on His life through us, His disciples.[15] We essentially serve the purpose of *becoming God's word* for those who have not yet learned to feed on the life and testimony of Jesus for themselves. As parents, *we* are the spiritual milk given to our children before they are able to drink from a cup and feed themselves. Just as they are dependent on us for physical food, so they are dependent on us for spiritual food. If they see us persevere during the good times and the bad, they will get a glimpse of the hope that God has set before them.

My daughter, Madeline, once made a statement that helped me realize just how much we are living ambassadors of God's Word to our children. She was about twelve-years-old at the time and had been going through extended bouts of illness in addition to bouts of anxiety from missing so much school. I was doing the same "mom walk" I had been doing for years, but this time, in addition to playing taxi driver, homework helper, and shoulder to cry on, I was also taking her temperature, making her smoothies, helping her get school assignments done, and encouraging her that things would eventually look up. Somewhere during this cycle, she stopped and said to me, "Mom, you are my wall. I can't stand without you."

What a statement.

In 2 Samuel 22:2, David refers to God as "my rock, my fortress and my deliverer," and being called "a wall" was close enough to make me momentarily proud. I was doing nothing out of the ordinary—just the stuff that loving moms try to do—but I was persevering as I was doing it, even though I was tired and felt like pooping out on my motherly duties. Madeline recognized this and gave me the best compliment possible by identifying me as her source of strength when she needed it. In this way, I temporarily became Christ to her. Later, she went on to recognize Christ Himself as her wall and source of strength.

Perseverance in parenting is truly priceless. No matter what you do or how down you get, never, ever give up! Hebrews 12:1 says it like this, "… let us throw off everything that hinders and the sin that so easily entangles. And let us run with perseverance the race marked out for us." By giving us our children, God has defined parenting as one leg of our race, so I'll say it again: never, ever give up! You can talk about how much you want to quit or think about how nice it would be to just drive away from the constant neediness of your children. You can take an evening or a day off—I highly recommend it!—but do not give up. You and your job are too important, and *you are not replaceable.*

When the Hot Springs Fail

As we persevere in our parenting, there will be times when we will need to get away to recharge. We may need to go to the beach for the day, or take a spa day and soak in some hot springs, as my friend, Diane, once did. She had reached her limit as wife and mom to a five-year-old with autism, so she took the day off in search of some mountain hot springs and spent the afternoon soaking. She felt better and I was impressed.

I can also relate. After a particularly chaotic and disappointing week at home, I asked Bryan to watch the kids (okay, I actually *told* him) and then flew out of the door. I got into my car, desiring to drive away to an exotic city and never return. It was a dramatic moment, much like in the movies, except I only went to Target. I am not as adventurous as Diane. Once I had left and driven around for a while, I realized I just needed an afternoon to myself to lollygag around the aisles and see the pretty things. After that I was fine to go home.

But what do we do in those times when Target or the hot springs do not provide a sufficient break? What if we have been working and/or praying to see an improvement in our child's issues with misbehavior, depression, or anxiety and there is little progress? What if we have been praying for years for our child to have a friend and we still see no result? What do we do with a child who feels abandoned by God because his or her prayers are not answered in the way he or she would like?

I have been through each of these problems. After much disappointment over the years, I have decided that I just have to be patient and realize God is not yet finished with me or my children. I have to believe that God loves us even if we do not always feel it. I have to remember that things will change as my children grow older, as life never ceases to evolve. Much like Paul described in 2 Corinthians 4:8, I might feel "hard pressed on every side, but not crushed; perplexed, but not in despair."

While we may not *yet* be able to say we can rejoice in suffering as Paul did (see Romans 5:3), we can look forward with confidence that God will somehow provide enough for us to carry on. He does provide, and we will be able to rejoice someday. After years of bearing my children's suffering, I can attest to this.

It can be easy to lose hope and want to give up when our children suffer with a trial for several years. A counselor with whom I once consulted helped me put this in perspective. He reminded me that the expected lifespan of Americans is approximately seventy years, and that later in life God's provisions can redeem even years of difficulty as a young person. All is not lost—even with a difficult childhood. Sometimes we get so caught up in the here and now that we forget the many years of joy that may still be in store for us and our children.

As parents, we have the advantage in knowing that life can improve after middle school and high school. If we are faithful, hopeful, and patient, we can offer wisdom and hope to our kids that are beyond their (and sometimes our) understanding. *We can become Christ* to our children for a little while, until they become old enough or mature enough to comfort themselves with His truths.

Letters from the King

In Isaiah 61:2-3, the prophet tells us that Jesus was sent to comfort "all who mourn," which includes our children who suffer and us as well, the caretakers of His precious children. Isaiah goes on to state that Jesus' ministry was to "bestow upon [us who mourn] a crown of beauty instead of ashes, the oil of gladness instead of mourning, and a garment of praise instead of a spirit of despair" (brackets added).

Clearly, God's words serve to comfort us in our mourning and sadness. It helps me to think of God's Word as His love letters to us. When we are separated from someone we love, the letters are comforting, even if the pain of separation continues. If we remember to soak in God's love letters to us, He provides an antidote to our grief until we are finally healed and reunited with Christ.

Let's also remember that without God, even the good things in this world will bring us grief—much like the Christmas letters I described at the beginning of this chapter. Although these letters were meant to bring friendly greetings from family and friends, they did not bring me joy. In fact, they actually served to increase my feelings of sadness and discontent.

Actually, it should not be surprising that man's creation of Christmas cards and letters often fails to increase our peace. They are not what God had in mind for us to spread the news of Christ and the freedom He brings. He knows our struggles require something more substantial than a cheery letter, text, or Facebook post. Rather, *His* newsy book, the Bible, acknowledges the grim reality of life by telling of the grim sacrifice that changed the world—because that is what it took. When we become discouraged over our parenting challenges and fail to see the blessings, the most effective way we can recharge and continue to persevere is to soak up *God's* Word and pay *less attention* to the words of others.

We need to believe God's Word when He promises to restore beauty to the ashes of our lives! James 5:11 tells us, "We count as blessed those who have persevered. You have heard of Job's perseverance and have seen what the Lord finally brought about. The Lord is full of compassion and mercy." As with Job, God doesn't always protect us from suffering, but He answers the prayers of those who mourn, and if we are faithful, He completes a good purpose in each of us and our children. Isaiah says we are "a planting of the Lord for the display of his splendor" (Isaiah 61:3). We are planted for a purpose. When we live in God's truth as people and as parents, we become powerful examples of grace and love, and others may risk putting their faith in Him as a result.

Perseverance *will* accomplish its purpose. So I will say it once again … never, ever give up!

8. In what areas of parenting are you tempted to give up?

_____

_____

_____

9. What about this discussion on perseverance motivates you to *not* quit?

_____

_____

_____

10. Write Isaiah 61:3 in the space below. What do you think God might be telling you about your *personal* mourning, or that of your child?

_____

_____

_____

Prayer Thought

God, it can be hard for me to remain focused on your truth when I am surrounded by the lies of this world. I thank you for the Holy Spirit who reminds me of the reality and values of my spiritual home. Please help me to listen to your truth, to believe it, and to act on this belief. Thank you for helping me persevere to see the fruits of my labor and the blessings you bestow on those who remain faithful. Amen.

Chapter 7

WHEN YOU GET UGLY:
HELP FOR PARENTS BEHAVING BADLY

It was like a scene from a horror movie. The woman, dripping wet and wrapped in a white bath towel, was stooped over and seemed to be clutching something in her hand. One child was hunched beneath her, cowering in fear, while the other looked on in terror and disbelief. Grimacing, the woman arched her arm and made repeated stabbing motions as though she were striking the huddled child over and over.

Was this a dream? No, actually, it was logical, gentle, and normally calm me, fresh out of the shower to break up a loud brawl between my teenage daughters. I was having a dramatic moment. I did *not* have a knife in my hand, but, yes, I was wildly acting out a stabbing scene over my children who were hitting and pulling each other's hair. What brought this on? Was I having a psychotic breakdown? No, I was just tired of having to break up fights between my girls. I was angry that I had to jump out of the shower to check on the fight scene, and I was frustrated that my words and attempts to physically separate them did not stop the brawl. Without even thinking about it, I resorted to the dramatic interlude.

Now, while I would not recommend this particular tactic for solving your children's squabbles, I have to say it worked beautifully. My children stopped dead in their tracks to watch their mother engaged in such an odd display. Later, I realized the only thing that might have been more effective is if I had dropped my towel and stood naked while mock-stabbing before them. Now *that* is the stuff of which horror movies are made! (Or at least some really good gossip.)

When Good Parenting Isn't Enough

Believe me, if you have any significant behavioral problems happening in your home, something like this is going to happen to you. While you may not take it to the dramatic extreme I did—I do have theatrical experience in my background—even the coolest cucumbers among us will at times transform into what seems like a green, frothing-at-the-mouth, Incredible-Hulk-type monster.

In a previous chapter, I wrote about how parenting disabled children can bring out the best in people, and how love can become more evident. However, the intensity and stamina required for this sort of parenting can also bring out the *worst* in us. Parenting our children is going to invite some situations into our lives that evoke strong emotion, and occasionally we might find ourselves displaying these emotions in odd ways. Some of the most kind and calm parents I know will admit to exhibiting hysteria, anger, frustration, and grief in a variety of public and private places.

Our emotional displays can often surprise us. I have shocked myself (and Bryan) by bawling at an Individual Educational Plan meeting at school, raising my voice at professionals, and growling like a caged animal at home. Almost all my friends with special-needs kids have done something similar. Really! I also went through a period in which I had to pray fervently for the will to keep from hurting my oldest daughter. Granted, the events taking place at the time were unusually intense. Katie was going through a phase in which she was hitting her younger sister several times a day, and I was intent on stopping this behavior.

At the time, Katie was about ten-years-old, and we had tried every parenting trick we knew. We had used techniques from the "best" parenting programs available, sought advice from counselors, and attempted to be as consistent in our discipline as possible. We had tried talking, time-outs, rewards, replacement behaviors and carefully controlled spanking. We had provided love, moral boundaries, prayer, support, structure, and stability. But it was not enough. We knew that Katie had an underlying disability that lowered her impulse control, but we were disappointed that none of these techniques had made a significant difference. We had even tried medicine, which proved to be helpful in many ways, but not with this particular problem.

Before I continue with the details of Katie's hitting phase and my parental response, let me cut to the happy ending. We finally brought in a behavior specialist who taught us how to restrain our daughter in a safe way until she could regain control of her emotions. It worked, and within weeks her hour-long rages decreased to just ten minutes. Several years later, they rarely ever occur for even a minute. There is hope!

Monster Parenting

In addition to this hitting problem, other behaviors exhibited by our children have pushed Bryan and me past textbook-perfect parenting. We have both become angry enough to lash out verbally or physically toward one of our daughters—something that will happen with most parents raising a child who does not follow social rules. This behavior did not work for us, nor is it a good parenting tactic for the long term. While this behavior might subdue a child for the moment, it also causes more anxiety and insecurity, which only serves to compound the original problem. During the months before Katie's behavior began to improve, Bryan and I both had to work hard on keeping our behavior calm and consistent. Once we had a plan that worked, our behavior improved as well.

Even when our behavior as parents is acceptable, our thoughts can convict us. After months of difficulty before our daughter's behavior improved, my thoughts about her began to change. Slowly it became more difficult for me to really *like* her. It was hard to separate her behavior from her personhood. Her aggression took the peace out of our home, and I was pulled into the role of a security guard or policewoman to keep the family safe. It was not fun and it was not the role I signed up for.

The thought that part of me did not like my oldest daughter was a strange realization, because I still *loved* her terribly. I would have done anything I could to help her. How could I feel this way? To be honest, after years of watching Katie's aggression and trying to protect others, I was just weary, frustrated, angry, and sad. I could see no good in the situation, and I could see no end to it. At that point, I began to understand how people could physically abuse their children. I was on the brink of doing it myself. What was happening to me? Why would a loving, calm, and responsible person like me have to struggle to restrain myself from hurting my own child? Was I becoming a monster?

I was not a monster; I was just struggling to maintain my emotional health in a difficult long-term situation. I was facing a serious problem, and all of my efforts to correct it had failed. I was somewhat isolated, with no nearby family to help me and no friends who could even fathom the situation. During this time, I prayed and read Scripture regularly so I could keep the strength to respond appropriately. Choosing the "appropriate" response was also difficult, as it depended on discerning the reason for poor behavior—was it disability, willful misbehavior, or both? As you may know, parenting is a more difficult job when the motive or origin for behavior is unclear.

For the record I have never abused my child, but this was an extremely humbling experience. I tell this story not to excuse any sort of child abuse but so you will realize an overly angry reaction can be a normal response to overwhelmingly difficult situations. Bryan and I are the last people on earth who you would expect to have such a struggle, but it happens in families like ours more than you might think. You can be a good parent, follow the best parenting advice available, and still feel out of control when your child is chronically acting out. The situation requires God's intervention and outside help. It can take several trials to find the right help for your family so it is important to recognize when your child's behavior cannot be helped with ordinary parenting techniques and to get help as soon as possible.

1. What are some situations that trigger your emotional or spiritual "ugliness" toward your child?

_____

_____

_____

Seeking Help

Katie began to decrease her aggressive behaviors once God provided help from a gifted behavior specialist. This specialist showed us a technique to carefully restrain (or hold) her in such a way as to contain her rage and prevent harm to her or any of us. This helped tremendously and greatly decreased the problems. Had we not received help at this time, we would have been forced to seek alternate solutions.

In our situation, the next step might have been to obtain live-in help so we could monitor our children constantly and still carry out the tasks of daily living. We could have separated our daughters by sending one to live with a relative, or we could have temporarily enrolled Katie in a live-in therapeutic facility. None of these options seemed right to us at the time, and we were thankful to find the solution that we did. However, many families have been forced to choose one of the other options in order to survive and keep other family members safe. Although it can be heartbreaking, seeking help can lead to a change in the child's behavior that ultimately keeps the family together.

2. What are some solutions you have found (or might want to try) to decrease the negative behaviors your child is exhibiting?

_____

_____

_____

Receiving the Blessings

Even though this was a difficult and troubling situation, our family did receive some blessings through the process. First of all, the entire family watched God provide solutions to help Katie control her anger. She is now a thoughtful young woman who remembers how God provided help to set her free from that burden. What a gift this is!

Second, God's Word helped me remain strong and obedient to do the right thing—at least most of the time—during that period. I learned to listen to His Spirit during critical moments when I had no idea what action to take, and to see the power in His suggestions. I am happy to give Him credit for the wisdom.

Finally, Bryan and I were blessed to learn that nobody is beyond acting in a sinful way when confronted with a really difficult problem. While we like to think of child abusers as a separate or lower class of people, this experience reminded us that we *all* have the potential for almost any kind of sin. It is humbling to realize how even educated, loving, God-fearing families can be pushed to the brink. This situation increased our compassion toward others and led us to find ways to help those who were experiencing similar problems.

Extent of the Problem

In case you are still feeling alone as you encounter behavior issues in your home, research reveals the prevalence of this problem. The National Institute of Mental Health (NIMH) regularly publishes reports that reveal the extent to which social, emotional, or behavioral challenges affect the children in our families. NIMH summarized a comprehensive 2010 study that reported the following statistic: "Just over 20 percent (or one in five) children, either currently, or at some time during their life, have had a *seriously debilitating* mental disorder".[16] This includes mood disorders such as major depression and bipolar disorder, anxiety disorders, conduct disorders, eating disorders, and attention deficit disorder (ADHD). This report also revealed that 46 percent of thirteen-to-eighteen-year-olds have suffered from some sort of mental illness at one point in their lives.

Another large national survey found that 13 percent of children aged eight to fifteen were diagnosed with a mental illness within the past year of that study (2004).[17] Other reports reveal that disorders such as Tourette's syndrome, autism spectrum disorders, post-traumatic stress disorder, and brain injury increase difficult or aggressive behaviors, and self-injury and substance abuse in children are on the rise. Given these findings, it is little wonder that increasing numbers of parents are in situations over which they feel they have little control. With this much of our population affected by social, emotional, or behavioral challenges, more and more people are experiencing distress in their families.

These stressors can trigger other kinds of unintentionally harmful parental behavior. For example, if parents have a child with a brain disorder or mental illness they do not know about or understand fully, they might tell their child to "pull it together," "toughen up," or "rise to the occasion." While encouraging our children to do their best is admirable, in some situations it may be physically impossible for the child to conform to his or her parents' expectations. This serves only to damage the child's already low self-esteem.

This scenario is typically played out in families in which a child has undiagnosed ADHD, depression, anxiety disorder, or early onset bipolar disorder. A child may appear to be lazy, disorganized, sloppy, unmotivated, or manipulative, when in reality the child is doing his or her best to overcome a chemical imbalance or other brain malfunction. Sometimes parents know the name of the diagnosis but have not read or researched it fully, so they still may have unrealistic expectations for their child.

Perhaps you have been guilty of handing out inappropriate accusations or exhortations to your child. If so, it is important for you to forgive yourself and move on. These problems and their solutions are rarely obvious or clear-cut, so everyone makes mistakes—professionals included. In addition, you cannot become an expert on a condition overnight, and nobody expects you to. You just need to keep learning, apologize if you were mistakenly hurtful, and continue forward.

Difficult People and Systems

While our child's behaviors may tempt us to behave badly, more often we will be provoked to anger and frustration by other people and systems as we seek help for our child. There are times when we advocate for what our child needs medically, in school, or in some other activity, but we are met with barriers and closed doors. In these situations, it is easy to become angry with insurance companies, medical professionals, mental health or disability systems, school administrators, teachers, coaches, or daycare providers who lack understanding and may be unable or unwilling to provide our child with what he or she needs.

Another type of ugliness many experience is feeling jealous toward other parents or children who seem to have it all together. Or, we may behave badly when we feel our extended family members do not understand our parenting experience and make inaccurate or insensitive comments. Every parent of a special-needs child I know can list hurtful, uninformed, and/ or insensitive statements made in regard to his or her parenting techniques. We can employ constructive ways to reduce this behavior in others, but ultimately we cannot control what other people say or do. We need to learn ways to express our negative feelings in a way that is not hurtful to others.

3. What situation triggers your "ugly behavior or thoughts" toward family, professionals, or strangers?

    _____

    _____

    _____

Getting Rid of the Ugly

All of these scenarios certainly provide reasons for us to be upset. It is true that services from school systems and other agencies we encounter are often far from perfect. It is also true that professionals, other parents, friends, and family members will do things that are foolish and will say things in ignorance. These offenses hurt and the wounds tend to linger. The question is how do we heal from these wounds to live in the freedom and joy God intends for us? In my twenty years of experience as a special-needs mom, only one thought has consistently helped me move past the negative effects of these actions and comments—that is to keep my focus on Christ and His example. I have found that the more I align my thoughts with biblical truth and seek to emulate Christ, the more I minimize the ugly and live with contentment and peace.

In this chapter, we will explore some actions (and their foundational truths) that reduce our bad behavior and help us live with contentment and peace. They are to (1) educate others, (2) advocate for our child, (3) retreat from "no-win" situations, and (4) forgive.

Educate

One way to prevent ourselves from getting trapped in angry thoughts is to educate those who are harmful in their ignorance. We even have a biblical precedent for this behavior. Although we may not always highlight Jesus' work as a teacher, it is true that a large focus of His work was educating others. He continually tried to *teach* the spiritually ignorant. In this endeavor, He found some of the people He encountered were stiff-necked and mean-spirited, but many were simply in the dark about life in the heavenly realm. Similarly, many people with whom we interact simply do not understand what living in our special-needs world is really like. Educating others is a productive course of action in many cases, and we should consider it as a first step when someone offends us or our child.

A common offense most of us can relate to often happens in the grocery store. As a matter of fact, almost every parent of a child with social, emotional, or behavioral problems I know has a grocery store story that causes festering anger. The stories focus around some foolish person who makes a rude comment when the challenged youngster whines, cries, talks back, or tantrums in some way. The individual usually says something like, "That kid really needs a good spanking," or something equally unenlightened. We are angered that (1) this person thinks he or she knows all about our child and our parenting skills, even though this may be our first encounter; (2) he or she actually has the gall to spout out his or her "wisdom" in the middle of a public place. Just who does this person think he or she is?

While our first inclination is to lash out, Scripture reminds us that we need to live at peace with everyone as much as possible (see Romans 12:17-19). This does not mean we have to accept the way everyone acts, but we are to try to choose a peaceful resolution to the problem. My friend, Gina, the parent of a special-needs child, came up with one solution by carrying with her a generous supply of "quick education cards." Whenever her child, Ethan, puts on a public show, she hands the cards out to people nearby. They are small—about the size of a business card—and simply describe Ethan's diagnosis and how it affects his behavior. Gina includes a quick explanation about what is usually the best way to extinguish the behavior and then lists a website for more information. Gina and other parents I know like this approach because it makes them feel vindicated from any judgments incurred, and ignorant people receive the message in a kind and calm way.

Other people in our child's life—such as family members, friends, coaches, and teachers—may need more information than what can be listed on a simple education card. For several years, I handed out two stapled sheets of notebook-sized paper that described Katie's diagnosis, some quirks or behaviors to expect, and the best way to handle those behaviors. I found this to be easier than trying to speak to every coach or teacher ahead of time. I also made sure to include my contact information for those who had questions. These information sheets protected both Katie and me from misunderstandings and took a lot of pressure off the people who were Katie's mentors for different activities. I have also recommended books and videos to family members and teachers who needed more information or who still seemed to be having trouble working with my child.

These solutions tend to work well with younger children who have outbursts or behavior quirks in public, but they may not work as well for a teenager with a more hidden disorder. My friend, Lorrie, has a seventeen-year-old daughter, Haley, with bipolar disorder. When Haley is in the depressive phase of her illness, her ability to fully participate in life is significantly dampened. However, those who are not close friends or family are often unaware of the problem. When Haley misses social events and people ask about her, Lorrie is often put in a difficult position. While she would like to explain her daughter's illness, she has to be careful with whom she discloses information, as she wants to preserve her daughter's privacy and avoid the associated stigma (see chapter 8). In the same way, as much as we need to work on fighting senseless stigma, we first have to be sensitive to our child's right to privacy. This especially becomes an issue when our children are adolescents and we want them to maintain their trust in us.

Outside of emergency situations, we need to ask our children for their permission to disclose personal information. We may need to give information only to a few close family members, friends, and others (such as teachers) who really need to know about the disability. As much as we would like the support and understanding of everyone we know, we may have to limit our disclosure until our child is ready to share.

4. In what ways could you educate others to help decrease your negative responses to their uninformed comments and behaviors toward your child?

_____

_____

_____

Advocate

Closely associated with educating others is advocating for our child. Not only is this good for our child, but it also keeps our mind on positive things when we are concerned about the people or environments that are affecting our son or daughter. However, caring for our child through advocacy efforts has the downside of often creating unintended enemies. The Bible exhorts us to take care of our family members (see 1 Timothy 5:4), but it also tells us to pray for our enemies (see Matthew 5:43-45). Get ready to start praying for those you encounter when you decide to advocate.

Advocacy gets a bad name because it often involves some type of confrontation. In many cases, advocacy causes parents to become "lawyers" for their child's cause. This is tricky to navigate, because it is easy for parents to get caught up in trying to outsmart or out-prove their "enemy." This is not exactly what we want to do as Christian moms and dads, and yet we will have to do it from time to time.

Advocacy is necessary because an important part of caring for our children is teaching them to live in society. Our children need to experience society at large, and most of these experiences will be helpful for their development. For children, this means teaching them how to function in some sort of school setting and in at least a few outside activities such as church, a social group, or a hobby group. If we find that our child is chronically uncomfortable, upset, or not making progress in one of these situations, it may be time to first educate and then advocate. What we need to learn is to advocate in a way that preserves the goodwill and good intent in our hearts.

A friend of mine was once faced with an advocacy situation with her daughter's middle school. During her sixth-grade year, her daughter, Emily, became anxious about going to class. She had struggled with anxiety for many years, but this was at a new level for her and she was feeling overwhelmed. She talked to her parents about it and repeatedly asked to stay home. My friend and her husband spoke with school staff to try to determine what was triggering Emily's anxiety, but the school personnel could not see the problem, and they claimed she was doing perfectly fine.

In response, my friend and her husband put on their advocacy hats and brought in documentation from a physician about their daughter's illness. This still did not change the school administrator's opinion, so in a third meeting my friend arranged for Emily's doctor to come in and explain that her daughter's anxiety was real and needed to be taken seriously. When this also failed to change the school administrator's understanding of the situation, my friend had to advocate for her child in several more highly pressured meetings until the school officials were willing to acknowledge the illness. Finally, the persistence paid off, and the school made small modifications to decrease her daughter's anxieties.

Of course, Emily's parents felt angry and dismayed about the school administrator's denial of their daughter's illness and her needs. Sometimes such disputes can be more serious, such as a family I know whose child was turned away from the county mental health department during an episode of hallucinations and suicidal behavior. It is true that many of our human systems do not work as well as they should, and it is easy to become furious with the system and those in authority. In this situation, it may become helpful to become involved in advocacy that can make a difference in changing the system. We can write letters describing policies that need to be changed, serve on policy committees, or march in rallies—whatever our preference.

In any advocacy situation, it can be tempting to become rude and downright ugly, or to at least harbor disdain against professionals or systems. We might be tempted to gossip about or slander those we perceive as having wronged our child or other children. While it is understandable to become angry in these situations, the Scriptures just remind us *not to sin* in our anger (see Psalm 4:4; Ephesians 4:26). We can share our negative experience in order to improve future services, but we must be cautious to share the information in a balanced and respectful way. We also need to recognize that what didn't work for our child in a certain school or treatment situation might work for another child in the same situation.

If we claim to be Christians, then we are ambassadors for Christ (see 2 Corinthians 5:20). This is serious business because what we say and do reflects upon Him. Jesus set the example of how to love our enemies (see Matthew 5:44), so we are to do the same. Sometimes we need to trust God to provide solutions for our problems in ways we have never even considered. If we do this, it is easier to treat others with respect and to concede some battles to those who disagree with us. I still believe that parents usually know what is best for their children and I encourage you to be assertive in sharing your ideas. However, it is also good to balance this with a humble heart. I have learned from experience that it can be more productive to give God some time to provide an unexpected solution than to immediately leave a pile of offended people in my wake. We also need to aspire to Jesus' example of a peaceful heart in spite of injustice (see Luke 23:34).

Fortunately, in my friend's situation with Emily and the school, she and her husband had learned from previous experience. Although it was hard for them to be sympathetic with the ignorance of the school personnel—especially after they made attempts to educate them—they were able to keep a reasonable relationship with the administrator and worked hard afterward to speak in a fair way about their experience. I know that other parents since then have enrolled their children with special needs at the same school and have had wonderful results.

In situations like this, recognize that while the ignorance of medical or school personnel is irritating, they are humans and fallible just like the rest of us. Our experience in educating and advocating within the system will help the next family who comes along. Realizing this as we go through the process can help prevent us from dwelling on the time and peace that have been needlessly taken from us. In addition, we need to remember that God looks out for all of humanity at the same time, and it is unrealistic for us to get our way every time. We have to trust that He has the situation in His hands, hears our prayers, and will lead us in the direction we need to go.

5. In what situations might advocacy help tame your negative thoughts and behaviors?

_____

_____

_____

Retreat

A third reasonable response to situations that continually anger us and put us into an ugly frame of mind is to remove our child or ourselves from the stressful environment. Now, I am not a quitter, and this response might sound like a cop-out. However, there are some circumstances in which this is the best approach. Let me elaborate.

There will be situations at school or in treatment situations where no matter what we do as parents to raise the quality of service for our child or other children, we will be met with a limited response. Many parents (including me) have faced this issue. To resolve the problem, we again need to try to educate, support the teacher or service provider in their efforts, and advocate for a more supportive environment. But if we do all this and the situation still does not improve, it is sometimes best to cut our losses and simply remove our child from that particular school, classroom, or other situation. This is not as easy to do in some areas of the country where there are limited options, but it is usually possible to remove our child from at least some sources of the problem, whatever they may be.

One situation in which making such a change—even when difficult—is the best course of action is when continuing to carry on in the same way will just cause more tension. Some situations will prove to cause us more grief than they are worth, and the time and energy we would spend in anger, planning, or worrying can be better used elsewhere. We all have limited energy, and if we spend it fighting the system to little avail, we will have less energy to parent our child to the best of our ability. For this reason, experienced parents agree that sometimes the cost of immediately changing the system is not worth the cost of bogging down their minds with continual irritation, anger, or frustration. We will experience enough of that just in parenting, and we need the extra brain cells to promote positive experiences with our child and family.

Another scenario in which retreating can be the best option is when we or our child is placed in a social situation that causes one of us increasing heartache. I have had experiences in which hanging out with my previously good friends no longer worked, because our parenting frames of reference had become so different that we could no longer relate in a mutually satisfying way. It has also happened that my children did not mesh with a friend's children, which also led to a diminishing friendship.

In such circumstances there is really no one to blame. It is just reality that we will tend to gravitate toward people who understand us. Oftentimes the hurt feelings, misunderstandings, and anger come *before* we realize a friendship is no longer working, so rather than stay in that situation, it is better to move on and find a better fit. I am not saying we have to abandon the friendship, but it might need to take on a different form—maybe one in which we meet for lunch occasionally, but not one in which the kids or families spend a lot of time together.

When we make the decision to retreat from a friendship—especially a previously strong one—we must recognize there will be a period of grief for the loss. We may feel a sense of sadness for being left out of a group or because we are no longer able to relate to it, but in time we *will* make new friends who will understand us better. In the long run, we will conserve our energy if we are not in situations that cause us perpetual negative feelings.

6. In what situations would retreating help with your negative thoughts and behaviors?

_____

_____

_____

Forgive

The final and most important step we can take to maintain a kind spirit is to continually seek God's help in forgiving those who have wronged us. Unfortunately, when we enter the world of parenting a child who falls outside the norm, we also enter a world of prejudice, fear, misunderstanding, and indifference. People who would normally be kind will often express their fearful self when encountering a person who is different. This means that sometimes even Christian parents who espouse loving others can become fearful and protective of their children—at the expense of ours.

I had to face this painful reality in my own life. My daughter, Katie, had made a Christian friend during her first year at a new high school. Samantha was kind and accepting, and she seemed to like Katie's personality and outlook on life. Katie appreciated Samantha as well and began to rely on her for moral support. Samantha's other friends, however, were less accepting, and they complained that Katie interfered with their group dynamics.

Over time, Samantha began to feel pressure from these friends to spend less time with Katie. Because Katie has autism, she did not pick up on Samantha's subtle hints to give her more time alone with her other friends. Finally, Samantha's mother, concerned with the pressure her daughter was feeling, talked to the school counselors and demanded that Katie completely divorce herself from talking to or interacting with her daughter at school. Her ultimatum was that if this didn't happen, she would take Samantha to a different school.

The most difficult part of this experience for me was that I knew Samantha's mom personally. We were both Christians, and she knew Katie had a disability and had been through a lot of rejection. But when it came to making this decision, her fears for her own child's adjustment overtook love in her thinking, and she chose to blackball my child. I do understand that parents are called to look out for the welfare of their children, but I found it difficult that this mom could not agree to compromise somewhere in the middle. I really needed God to help me forgive her action.

In this situation, it helped me to remember that Jesus was unfairly treated, misunderstood, and wounded, yet He did not live with bitterness in His heart. This was true even when He faced His death upon the cross (see Luke 23:34). He was and is amazing. If Jesus forgave those who sought to kill Him, certainly He will help me forgive the hurt my daughter and I experienced in our past and in the future.

In 1 John 4:18, we are told that "perfect love drives out fear." How wonderful it would be if we could all learn to allow God's perfect love to cast out our fears. But even when we are wronged because of others' fears, we can rely on this perfect love to enable us to forgive them (see Ephesians 4:32). I know I have been a fearful mother myself and have undoubtedly wounded other people with my actions. With God's grace, I hope to respond—at least the next time—with love and not fear.

7. Is there someone you need to forgive to allow you to have more positive and productive thoughts? If so, how might you start this process?

_____

_____

_____

Be Part of the Solution

As I conclude this chapter, the principle I want you to take away for keeping yourself from acting ugly in your own pain and fear is this: Do your best to *educate, advocate, retreat (if necessary), and forgive* often. Making progress in these areas will enable you to be part of the solution rather than the problem. It reminds me of a Chinese proverb I adopted as my motto early in my special-needs parenting journey: "It is better to light a small candle than to curse the darkness." Remember that God is always there to help light your candle and keep it burning when you feel the darkness creeping in.

8. Isaiah 26:3 tells us that God "will keep in perfect peace him whose mind is steadfast, because he trusts in [Him]" (brackets added). How would your feelings about your circumstances change if you were to continually focus on your trust in God and His love?

_____

_____

_____

9. How can you make this steadfast focus on God a practical reality in your life? (Be specific.)

_____

_____

_____

Prayer Thought

Dear God, I am easily insulted, wounded, and fearful, especially in my dealings with those whose actions affect my children. Help me to acknowledge Your wisdom when I am tempted to react in ways that displease You. Help me to choose my words and actions wisely, and only after consulting with You. Remind me that You love my "enemies" just as You love me, and help me learn to think from Your holy perspective. Amen

Chapter 8

WHAT ABOUT ME?
FINDING ABUNDANCE IN SACRIFICE

I f you have been the parent of a special-needs child for any length of time, I am sure you have had a moment where you dreamed about getting in the car for an evening out—and never coming back. Certainly you love your children, but the constant demands and intensity can lead to caregiver fatigue or burnout. Sometimes there seems to be no escape, and you might feel trapped, smothered, and weighed down by the tasks in the days ahead.

At least several times a year I find myself ready to give up. I tell Bryan that I want a new job—I no longer like the one I have of caring for the house and kids, and everything it entails. Sometimes I drive around town hoping to think of another errand that will keep me from facing my teenage girls, who lately have been making valiant efforts to avoid, forget, or fight their way out of household chores. They also tend to squabble … loudly. Why would I want to go home to another sibling joust when I could wander around the mall and see the fancy sights? It makes me seriously entertain thoughts of offering room and board to a super-nanny who could teach the children, make scrumptious dinners, and do the housework and laundry. In the meantime, I could zip off in stylish pumps to do the glamorous work of stamping out pain and difficulty in the lives of unfortunate souls who live in challenging situations like myself.

Sadly, the work of parenting a child with special needs is neither glamorous nor pump friendly. It is best done in the trenches of home, and that is where I have always returned. Some days are frustrating as I attempt to teach my two children how to clean the house, manage their time, and learn the ethic of "work first, play later." The task requires a Herculean effort and a conviction that it really is an important lesson to teach. Sometimes it requires a loud voice to match my daughters' and a stubborn tenaciousness. It demands a sacrifice of time and energy that I would rather spend on other things.

All diligent parenting requires some degree of sacrifice—sacrifices in sleep, financial resources, and free time. For parents and family members of special-needs children, however, it requires additional sacrifice. As I have mentioned, in my case it meant postponing the completion of my doctoral degree, and once I finished that, it meant not even attempting a full-time career. It has meant advocating and working on behalf of my children to the point I experienced chronic fatigue. It has meant turning over the direction of the non-profit organization I founded to someone else so I could be more available for my children. More recently, it has again meant putting aside my personal goals to place my youngest daughter in a homeschool program.

Counting the Cost

Consider the kinds of sacrifices your family has made. Have you given up a promotion or job so you could be more available for your child? If you have not sacrificed your career in some way, you have probably sacrificed much of your free time or hobbies. Most all your time is likely spent working at your vocation, helping with homework, transporting your child to appointments, engaging in therapeutic activities, or actively trying to negotiate behavioral problems. I know parents who have lost their jobs because they needed to take off too much work time to care for their child. Other parents have increased their work hours or taken a second job to pay for therapeutic services. This includes parents whose children are young and those whose children are adults.

Extended family members of a special-needs child also have to make sacrifices. Sometimes grandparents become caregivers because the parent or parents need to work. Siblings of special-needs children often give up their preferences or choices of activities because the child with social, emotional, or behavioral problems has a more limited ability and/or willingness to engage. The other child can resent this role.

Years of these kinds of sacrifices can be emotionally difficult, and over time it is likely we will experience feelings of resentment because our children require so much of our time and energy. If we are stay-at-home parents, we might resent our spouses who continue with their careers while we sacrifice our own for the duties of special-needs child rearing. Even if we make a well-informed choice to put our children's needs above our own, it can still be difficult.

In this chapter, we will examine how to handle these sacrifices without becoming bitter, self-absorbed, isolated, lonely, or out of touch with the rest of life. We will look at some ways to appropriate time for our spouse and other children and to keep from feeling trapped in our roles as caretaker and advocate for our special-needs child. We will address how mothers often feel the need to be everything to everyone, and will touch on the specific needs of spouses and siblings. By the end of this chapter, it is my hope that we will each have a better understanding of our freedom in Christ and how to find balance as we care for our kids.

1. What are you sacrificing now for the sake of your child?

_____

_____

_____

2. How do you feel about this sacrifice? Are you experiencing joy and satisfaction in knowing you are making a good choice, or are you feeling some resentment about it—or both? Explain.

_____

_____

_____

Love and Sacrifice

As we make personal sacrifices for our child, our highest priority is to avoid feeling bitter and resentful. For me, a key to keeping a loving spirit during a long period of suffering is to understand that *real love is all about sacrifice.* Like most life lessons, we learn this as we mature spiritually and emotionally. For instance, when we first fell in love with our spouse, it is unlikely that sacrifice played a large part in our courtship. Most of us were young and somewhat immature, and we understood love to mean the happy feelings we experienced when our loved one walked into the room and we spent time with him or her. In most situations, the biggest sacrifice we made was to give up a job or school enrollment so we could live in the vicinity of our spouse. Later, we may have made sacrifices in order to get along with in-laws or provide for our families.

Real love is all about sacrifice.

The introduction of a child into a marriage pushes open the envelope of sacrifice. Changing dirty diapers and staying awake with a sick infant quickly thrusts new parents into an expanded definition of love. However, the rewards gained from raising children usually mitigate feelings of resentment from all the extra work required. I am convinced this is one of the reasons why God made babies so cute. However, if the child is not looking so cute lately and is not giving back many rewards to his or her parents, the scale becomes unbalanced and resentment creeps in.

Whether or not we realize it, we expect positive feedback from our children in return for everything we have done for them. It is normal to expect "good childing" (see chapter 6). However, what we consider good childing will look different at every stage of development, and what we consider rewarding will vary. We may feel rewarded by a smart child, or by an attractive, compliant, athletic, or outgoing one; or we might be fine with a child who gives us a simple "thank you" or a hug and kiss. But when the child does not meet these expectations or express much affection, we learn the real meaning of parental love: to accept our child for who he or she is rather than demand a more self-gratifying type of child. We learn true love's patience and kindness.

First Corinthians 13 is a well-known poetic chapter in the Bible that is often read at weddings. However, God intended us to apply the concepts in this passage daily to all of our relationships, including those with our children. I like the translation of this "love chapter" as it is often called, in the New King James Version. In verse 4, Paul states, "Love suffers long and is kind." These six words speak volumes. If we love someone, we will "suffer long" for them. Period. If we are not willing to suffer long for the sake of someone, maybe it is not love we feel, or maybe we are too immature to move into this kind of love. In verse 11, Paul writes, "When I was a child, I spoke as a child, I understood as a child, I thought as a child; but when I became a man, I put away childish things." Are we willing to put away our childish thoughts of love and exhibit mature loving behavior? Are we willing to "suffer long" for our child with social, emotional, and behavioral challenges and do the right thing for the sake of love?

Long-suffering, patience, and sacrifice are not an easy calling. We want to say, "Hey, what about me? What about my life, my dreams, my plans?" I have had these questions myself throughout my parenting years. While I love my children sacrificially, I am not always willing to accept the sacrifice without complaining, whining, or engaging in self-pity. Transitioning from childish to adult thinking has been a struggle. But through the struggle, I have gained understanding of true love.

The last verse in 1 Corinthians 13 is meaningful to those of us who are raising a child with social, emotional, or behavioral challenges and to people who are experiencing all sorts of trials. In this verse, Paul writes, "And now abide faith, hope and love, these three; but the greatest of these is love" (NKJV). In the first chapter of this book, we explored how faith and hope are crucial to our development and functioning as parents of special-needs kids. But, as Paul states, love is even greater.

Jesus demonstrated this triad of faith, hope, and love with perfection. He showed faith in His Father's plan, hope for Himself and for mankind, and He made the ultimate sacrifice of love on the cross. In Matthew 26:64, we see Jesus' faith in God's plan of redemption when He states, "I say to all of you: In the future you will see the Son of Man sitting at the right hand of the Mighty One and coming on the clouds of heaven" (see also Mark 14:62). Jesus had a hope—an *expectation*—of sitting at God's right hand and being with His followers in heaven.

But as much as Jesus exhibited faith and hope, *He is best known for His sacrificial love.* The hallmark verse of the Christian faith is John 3:16: "God so loved the world that he gave his one and only Son, that whoever believes in him shall not perish but have eternal life." Unfortunately, this verse can become so familiar to us that we overlook its impact and example for our lives—that God and Jesus are the ultimate models of sacrificial love. In 1 Corinthians 13, Paul tells us that love is the greatest and longest-lasting attribute that we can attain. Do we take this seriously? Do we attempt to exhibit love in all we say and do? Are we willing to demonstrate love by our actions instead of with just our words?

It helps to remember that our sacrifice of time, career, or ambition is nothing more than a demonstration of love for our children. It is not a strange ritual practiced by only the most religious in society, or something that others should laud as exceptional. It is simply love in action. If we are Christians this type of sacrificial love is expected of us. It does not make us martyrs or saints of extraordinary proportion, but we should feel good about learning how to love more like Christ because it pleases God. We should also feel good about loving our children the best we can so that we can look back without regrets.

Societal vs. Godly Expectations

Even if we know that God wants us to exhibit sacrificial love, it is not popular in American society. Our culture tells us that it is too much, over the top, or otherwise unhealthy. We are discouraged from sacrificing too much of ourselves, especially as women and mothers. This idea probably has roots in the equal-rights movement on behalf of women. I fully support equal rights for women, but in reality it can be difficult for women to "have it all" (that is, a fulfilling career, a happy marriage and a satisfying family life). The truth is that in situations where a family has a child or children with social, emotional, or behavioral challenges, maintaining a balance on the "happy" side usually requires a lot of extra work and time from the parents (especially the mom). Living close to supportive extended family can help fill the gap, but if there is no such assistance available, the extra time and effort has to be pulled from somewhere. The question we must ask ourselves is which area in our life will be sacrificed.

As much as I have participated in and been a proponent of higher education, I believe many colleges and universities have failed their graduates by ignoring the reality of human limitations. Students are taught to be successful professionals without having the conversation of what sacrifices will be required to achieve this. Secular and Christian universities alike emphasize achievement over love and service. They may claim to promote service, but they usually do this in the context of achieving a level of public service, not private, behind-the-scenes service. As a rule, colleges are a reflection of the popular culture, and the one in which we live promotes success.

Of course, it would be inaccurate to accuse all colleges and professors of lauding achievement over service. Jon Johnston, a professor at Pepperdine University, is one notable exception. In his book *Christian Excellence: Alternative to Success*, he compares and contrasts the realities of "success" versus "excellence."[18] The following chart summarizes some of his principle tenets.

Success	Excellence
Offers a hoped-for future goal	Provides a striven-for present standard
Bases our worth on a comparison with others	Gauges our value by measuring ourselves against our own potential
Grants rewards to the few, but is the dream of the multitudes	Available to all living things, but is accepted by few
Focuses its attention on the external	Focuses its attention on the internal spirit
Engenders fantasy and striving for the pot of gold at the end of the rainbow	Brings us to reality and a deep gratitude for the affirming promises of God
Encourages expedience and compromise, which prompts us to treat people as means to our ends	Cultivates principles and consistency, which ensure we will treat all persons as intrinsically valuable—the apex of God's creation

Even if we do not struggle with sacrificing success to care for our child, Johnston's principles are valuable because they show us the difference between godly excellence and worldly success. This is critical for fully accepting our child, because it is less likely that he or she will be successful in the worldly, high-achieving sort of way. Although there are certainly exceptions, many children with serious social, emotional, and behavioral challenges often do not achieve great status or clout, as they are using their energy elsewhere. However, they may become *excellent* people, which is much better.

I put forth these principles to encourage each of us to be strong enough in our faith and values to do what is right for our loved ones and our families, even at the expense of success and even when we know it will decrease our status or *perceived* importance in the world. Excellence, as defined here, reminds us of our real purpose in life: to love God and love one another. Of course, the decision to love others and prioritize their needs loses its value if we play the martyr or want to receive kudos for our dedication. Achieving excellence means serving without thought to recognition.

3. How can your own expectations or others' expectations add to your feelings of resentment over your need to sacrifice? Are you seeking success or excellence in your life?

_____

_____

_____

As we seek to serve our loved ones instead of feeding our own careers or personal interests, we must remember that the world's negative *perceptions* of our choice will not represent the truth. The world's perceptions are based on certain beliefs and thoughts, which may or may not be accurate. This is a lesson the late Mother Teresa knew well. She put little or no value on what the world thought and chose instead to value God's perceptions. She began her work simply because she felt privileged to share God's love with the sick and dying. She never claimed to have great wisdom, prowess, or ability to be God's hand of love—she just did what she could and gave her time and energy to serve. This is the definition of true excellence. Mother Teresa knew that God was pleased with her actions, and that was enough. Ironically, it was this humble attitude that made her one of most famous Christian servants in modern history, and it eventually earned her the Nobel Peace Prize. Even more importantly, it earned her the approving nod of God.

Like Mother Teresa, we need to remember that any kind of loving action or sacrifice on behalf of our child is God's work. If we find ourselves homeschooling our child, advocating at our child's school, decreasing (or increasing) our hours at work, or on the floor playing childish games for more hours than we would like, we should rejoice in the fact that our actions are demonstrations of love and that we are exactly where God wants us to be. We will never be more in the center of God's will for our lives than when we love another person at our own expense. Of course, this does not mean we become the brunt of another person's abusive behavior, but rather that we do what we can to ease the pain of others. This is the story of the gospel.

> Any kind of loving action or sacrifice on behalf of our child is God's work.
>
>

We know in theory that love produces beautiful results, but it does not always look so pretty in action. Jesus' death on the cross certainly did not look pretty, though it was the most beautiful act ever demonstrated. Your tired face after a night consoling a distraught child will certainly not look pretty either, but God will see it as beautiful and excellent. In due time, you and your child will see that beauty as well.

4. How does this idea of linking love and sacrifice change your perception of your situation? Does it help to ease your feelings of resentment? If so, how?

_____

_____

_____

Three Practical Pointers

Ultimately, there is no permanent sting from sacrifice because what we are doing is beautiful in God's eyes. Like an insect bite, the sting is temporary; it is painful, red, and itchy at first, but then it gradually lessens and demands less of our attention. However, just as we would put ice and ointment on an insect bite, it is good to have a few pain relievers for the initial sting of sacrifice. Here are three pointers that can help you and your family handle periods of sacrifice with grace.

First, during periods of sacrifice, continue to seek meaningful social interaction with friends and loved ones. By maintaining these relationships, you can avoid cycles of self-isolation that lead to loneliness, depression, frustration, anger, and resentment. Becoming isolated from enjoyable friendships only increases the chance that resentment will become a normal part of your thought cycle. Taking the time to meet a friend for coffee or for a walk each week can provide an amazing attitude adjustment. Put these outings on your calendar just as you would set aside time for work or medical appointments.

Second, spend at least one hour each week doing something you really enjoy. Even taking fifteen minutes a day to putter in the garden, read a book, or sip a favorite cup of coffee will give you something positive to anticipate. This will lessen your feelings of deprivation during periods of sacrifice and increase your effectiveness when you return to parenting. Finding regular intervals to enjoy life will prevent resentment from building up within you, which is especially important during family crises. Do not neglect to take time for yourself each day.

Third, whenever your child is not giving you the thanks or positive feedback you desire, consider taking a moment to look at his or her baby pictures. This may sound silly, but it can spur loving feelings for your child when he or she is acting less than lovable. The resulting feelings can then motivate you to again persevere in caring for your child.

On Siblings

Entire books have been written to help parents understand and support siblings of special-needs children. While I cannot go into such detail in this book, it would be remiss for me to ignore this subject completely. For this reason, I want to share a few commonsense pieces of advice that most experts agree can help siblings of special-needs children cope with the stress they experience in their families.

First, experts agree it is important to budget ten to fifteen minutes of uninterrupted one-on-one time with each of your children and your spouse on a daily basis. Siblings of children with special needs often get overlooked in the chaos of family life, so it is critical to set aside some special time with them each day. This is especially important because siblings will often not recognize the disabilities in their brother or sister (unless it involves severe limits on normal self-care and intellectual functioning) and will become resentful if they perceive their brother or sister is getting special attention or fewer consequences for their misbehavior. When parents fail to give attention to the children without special needs, it only adds fuel to their existing negative feelings. You will be amazed at how spending even a short period of quality time with them will contribute to feelings of connectedness and keep them feeling loved and appreciated.

Experts also agree that siblings of children with special needs have to be given the opportunity to freely express their feelings toward their sibling—even if those feelings are negative. Siblings may vacillate between feelings of anger, loss, and grief concerning the special-needs child (just as parents do), so they need to be able to talk openly about these feelings to at least one parent. If the child feels that he or she has to bottle up emotions, it will only strengthen his or her resentment and cause a whole new set of problems.

If you, as a parent, find that you are unable to listen to a sibling's complaints without verbalizing disapproval or correction, you may need to find a counselor or friend who can accept these feelings. While it is important to encourage your children to love their siblings unconditionally and empathize with their difficult situations, this needs to be done in small steps as children progress in age and maturity—and only *after* the sibling has been able to freely express his or her feelings. While you do not have to agree with your child's thoughts or beliefs, you do not have the right to dismiss his or her emotions.

On Your Spouse

In regard to your spouse, I know it is easy to think that he or she is an adult and needs to take care of him or herself while you pour out your energy to care for the special-needs child and his or her siblings. While you should be able to expect more maturity and patience from your spouse, neglecting the relationship altogether will put it in jeopardy. It is critical that you do not neglect date nights and uninterrupted time with your spouse. He or she is your most important ally as you go through periods of personal sacrifice, so you need to keep this relationship as strong as possible during difficult times with your child. While it is easy for married couples to fall into the habit of picking on each other during tough times, you need to remember you are on the same team—and then act like it. When stressful events build in our home, Bryan is good at reminding me of this truth. If I start to get grumpy with him over an underlying frustration with our children, he will say, "Hey, I'm on your team here." It is almost always enough to calm me down and reframe my thinking.

One of the most important moves you can make to survive a sacrificial season is to find some form of respite for your special-needs child so you can spend some time away with your spouse. Children with neurological challenges will stress even the strongest and most mature marriages, so it is vital to take an occasional respite in the form of a retreat or vacation to communicate your respect and appreciation for one another. Taking a marriage enrichment class can also contribute to keeping your marriage strong during seasons of stress and sacrifice. Whatever you choose, remember that you are going through a *season* of sacrifice—and that you want to have a good marriage when the season is over.

Practical Points for Moms Who Try to Do Everything

The role of primary caregiver for the children in a family often falls to the mom. If the mom is responsible, caring, and committed to the family's well-being, the demands of caring for a child with social, emotional, or behavioral challenges can flip her into a sorry state. While I praise moms who prioritize their families, make sacrifices, and work diligently for their child's welfare, there will be times when they won't be able to fix their child's problem in a simple or timely manner—and working harder to do so will only lead to burnout. To cope with this reality, see the following additional tips for caregivers.

Accept Your Limitations

First, as the parent of a child with special needs, accept that you cannot be everything to everybody all the time—and that trying to do so won't be good for either you or the recipients of your help. As much as you might want to solve all of your child's problems, it won't be possible for you to do so. There are some lessons you can't teach—lessons that can only be learned through the School of Hard Knocks (see chapter 6). It can be difficult to let go and watch your children stumble, but it is better for them to experience small failures when they are young so you can be there to comfort and advise them. If their first failures happen when they are adults, it will be much more difficult for them to pick up the pieces. Failure with support can be a wonderful teaching tool.

> Accept that you cannot be everything to everybody all the time.

Accept That You Cannot Control Everything

Control is something most people strive to obtain, as it makes them feel competent and secure. However, even with sacrifice and your best efforts, you will not be able to control everything that happens to your child. For this reason, you need to understand that while it is noble to sacrifice your time and energy to help your kids find some mastery over theirs, there is a limit to your ability to control the outcome. You have to be content with making a valiant effort and not letting results be the only measure of your success.

When my children were young, I made a pledge to have no regrets regarding my parenting. This does not mean I did everything perfectly, but just that I promised to do my best based on what I knew and what I could do at the time. Likewise, if you do your best within your circumstances, you have done all you can. Great confidence also comes through taking all your concerns to God in prayer and asking Him for wisdom as you make decisions and care for your child.

Avoid the Blame Game

Along this journey with your special-needs child, it is inevitable that someone will make a mistake concerning the diagnosis, treatment, or advice they give you to support your child. Feeling upset about these mistakes is understandable, but it is important to forgive these imperfect people. It is convenient to blame doctors, the medical system, the school system, and/or unsupportive family members for the problems you face, but blaming others takes the love out of your sacrifice and turns you into a whiner. It will also destroy your peace. If you find it difficult to let go of your anger over the mistakes of others (or your own mistakes), consider seeking help from a counselor or friend, and pray consistently over this problem. This will help you separate whining from positive action.

Be Grateful

Especially during difficult seasons, it is important to be grateful that you love someone enough to sacrifice for him or her and that *you are needed* for this service. Your life will be well lived if you serve in this way. It may be that caring for your child is one of the ways God is preparing you or someone around you for a great work. In the Bible, both Mary and Elizabeth had to sacrifice much in their parenting of Jesus and John, respectively, and endure great losses. They were ordinary women who parented for God's greater purposes, but that did not excuse them from tremendous pain when both sons were despised and later executed. Let's look at their stories in some detail.

Mary had a rough start to her pregnancy in the first place, yet she accepted God's plan (see Luke 1:38). Maybe some of you can relate to this. God ordained her to become pregnant as an unwed mother, but her friend Elizabeth, who "was filled with the Holy Spirit ..." proclaimed

Mary to be "blessed among women" (Luke 1:41-42). As faithful Jewish women, it is likely that Mary and Elizabeth were familiar with Isaiah's prophecy of a suffering savior, so they might have guessed what was to come. Even if they didn't make this connection, they had to feel uncertain about parenting these atypical children. Still, they were honored to be part of God's larger plan.

If this example is not enough to encourage your thankfulness, obedience to God is an even better reason. In 1 Thessalonians 5:18, Paul reminds us to "give thanks in all circumstances, for this is God's will for you in Christ Jesus." How's that for clarity? Even though it sometimes seems impossible to give thanks like this, I have recently learned the amazing value of doing just that. I have learned to thank God for situations that seem less than ideal, trusting that He knows best. As a result, joy tends to follow in a miraculous way.

Don't Buy into the World's Lies

Sometimes, your sacrifice and efforts may stem from a concern that you need to "fix" your children's problems so they can go forward to become productive members of society. Contributing to society is great, but do not buy into the lie that productivity equals worth. You (and I) need to remember that people with disabilities contribute much to God's greater purposes. Those who recover enough to share their hope-filled stories are among the most inspiring people in the world, while those who do not recover point us to the hope of heaven. The truth is that it is a privilege to be part of the training and nurturing of any child in God's kingdom.

Do Not Grow Weary in Doing Good

A final point to consider is that raising your child will offer you the opportunity to do good, even if it is difficult. In any situation, all of us have the opportunity to bless others. Paul states in Galatians 6:9, "Let us not become weary in doing good, for at the proper time we will reap a harvest if we do not give up." You may or may not see a physical reward for your efforts during your lifetime, but the promise in this passage speaks to a spiritual harvest that you will receive as you live your life in God's presence.

5. What are some areas in your life in which *balancing* care for your special-needs child, your other children, your spouse, and yourself tends to get out of kilter?

_____

_____

_____

6. What practical steps can you take to restore balance?

_____

_____

_____

_____

Finding God's Rest

Part of the spiritual reward we receive for our sacrifice is entering into God's rest—and how wonderful it is! Of all life's necessities, sleep is the most important—medical research is clear that people cannot live without it for more than a few days. Rest is truly a blessing. As Hebrews 4:9 reveals, "There remains, then, a Sabbath-rest for the people of God; for anyone who enters God's rest also rests from his own work, just as God did from his."

My friend, Cathy, who parents a child with autism, once told me about a dream she had. In the dream, everyone in her family had been taken hostage, and it was up to her to free herself and save everyone. This dream could easily have been mine (and maybe yours), as I spent many nights in fitful sleep, worrying about how I would be ready for any needs my children might have. Clearly, it is hard to rest in this state of hyper vigilance.

Most of us rest just enough to survive so we can continue to be alert on behalf of our children. We seem to sleep with one ear and eye open in case of emergency. But God's rest is so much better. To me, a paraphrase of scriptural references to God's rest could be summarized like this: "Don't worry about a thing, for I, the Master of the universe, have your cares and concerns under My control. Nobody has a problem that I cannot fix. You have labored, and now is your time of rest. Enter it with joy and thanksgiving." This is the spiritual harvest we inherit. Praise God!

7. Write out Hebrews 4:9. How can you access God's rest as a reward for your efforts?

_____

_____

_____

_____

Prayer Thought

Lord, as a parent of a special-needs child, I can become consumed with trying to fix every situation. I sometimes feel resentful when I must limit other activities to provide the special care to meet my family's needs. These efforts can lead to exhaustion and disappointment when my plans do not succeed as I expect. Help me to surrender my plans to You so that I may balance work and rest. Allow me to enter into Your perfect rest. Amen.

Chapter 9

WHAT YOUR CHILD REALLY NEEDS AND HOW TO GIVE IT

I'm continually impressed by how much thought and effort moms (and dads) exert to benefit and bless their children. As parents, we would do most anything for them. We find out what they need and leap major hurdles to help. I am no exception.

When my oldest daughter, Katie, was ten-years-old, the idea of starting an organization to help her and other children began to form in my mind. She had been part of a group that was focused on developing social and emotional skills in children with autism spectrum disorders, but it was about to end. I wanted something like it to continue, so I gathered a group of like-minded parents and started SLATE. A year later, we ran our first training program for children with autism. We called it Get S.E.T. (Social Emotional Training), and it was—and continues to be—a great success.

For about a year prior to the start of this program, I volunteered an average of twenty hours per week to get it up and running so it could serve my child and fourteen other children. It really met a need in the community. Parents were thrilled, and I was so glad to have created something that would help not only my child but other children in the community as well. The only problem was that when the program began the next summer my own daughter hated it. Her state of mind did not sync with the program, and it resulted in many tears and behavior challenges.

Never one to accept defeat without a good fight, I garnered outside help and set up a special smaller group within the program to try to meet her needs. I desperately wanted her to stay in the program and reap the benefits. However, about two-thirds of the way through, she was still having great difficulty, so I admitted defeat and pulled her out. While I was going out three days a week to help other kids with autism in a specialized program, my own daughter stayed at home with a sitter. As you can imagine this was a major disappointment for me.

When Best Efforts Are Not Enough

As this story demonstrates, even when we think we know what our children need, sometimes our best efforts are not enough to provide it. As parents, if we cannot cure the particular cause of the disability, we at least want to lessen the effects as much as possible. If we cannot do this we wonder what we *can* do. Where is our time best spent? Will these efforts be good enough? Even without clear answers to these questions, we will usually try many things to help our children. And, to our credit, some of these efforts can be very creative.

For instance, we might try homeschool, therapeutic school, private school, or integrating our children into a local public school. We may train peer mentors and home helpers to be quasi-therapists. Most of us will enroll our kids in sports, music lessons, drama, youth group, Bible study or a variety of other activities and try to garner the proper support to make these activities successful. We will visit the recommended professionals, join support groups, lead support groups, or even develop programs to help our child. It is also common for parents to try special diets, supplements and medication, and to support exercise for the health of the whole family. We can be committed to taking care of ourselves, as well, in order to be the best we can be to keep all the plates spinning. I mean, seriously, our efforts can be impressive.

This list just scratches the surface of what is possible to try and what many of us have done. There is so much we can do, but often our efforts still seem to fall short of what is needed. We might wonder what is really enough. In many situations a cure is not likely, so the bulk of our efforts is directed toward managing problems to give our children the best life possible. Unfortunately, sometimes our kids need more than we can give. Every family is different, but in each there are limitations as to what parents can provide. We might have limits on how much emotional energy, intellect, time, or financial support we can give. We might not have access to the best specialists or programs in our child's area of need. Or we may have access to the specialists, but our child refuses treatment. We may not have helpful relatives or a support group nearby.

Even if we provide a near-perfect environment and the best therapies possible, our child can still have social problems, emotional outbursts, lack of focus, depression, or poor behavior. This can be so discouraging. How are we to respond? If we cannot give our child everything, what can we do?

1. What are some things that you are unable to fix for your child right now?

   _____

   _____

   _____

2. How do you feel about this?

   _____

   _____

   _____

Love and Parenting

Over the years I have known the frustration involved in my inability to fix everything. I remember a dear friend telling me as a young mom that my job was just to *love* my children and not to fix all of their problems. This advice was good and the words sounded so freeing, until I began to try to distinguish love from helping fix the problems—and I was stumped again. What does loving our children really mean? Isn't helping our children part of love?

The answer to that question is "yes." On a practical level, we inherently know that love means caring for our child's physical and emotional needs as best we can. It means teaching and helping him or her to know and love God and obey His commandments. But is more required in our special-needs parenting situation? Does love mean learning the best parenting techniques and securing the best therapies? If so, which are the best? And what if we cannot be sure of the reason for our child's actions? How can we then choose the correct approach?

All of the uncertainties can be mind-boggling, and they will continue as our children enter young adulthood. We will also encounter conflicting advice. Some people will encourage us to let our kids learn from their mistakes. Others will say we need to intervene very directly to prevent and correct the mistakes. In truth, both methods work at different times and in different situations, and I have spent time in both camps. Other questions that may come up are: How much time and energy should we spend to help our kids succeed? What limits should we put on parental intervention as our children age? How do we know when enough is enough? In truth, we may never know, although parenting programs and counselors can often make it sound as if there are sure answers. The answers to these questions are very situation and person specific, and there is *not one best solution* for everyone. The only sure answer is to direct our questions to God and to know that He will keep His promise to give us wisdom when we ask.

3. What are some uncertainties you have about your attempts to help your child?

_____

_____

_____

Have you prayed about these concerns?

_____

The Covering of Love

In the midst of uncertainty, I am so thankful that God's Word will always help us find wisdom for the questions in our lives. In my own struggles as a parent, I have been comforted many times by 1 Peter 4:8, which says, "Above all, love each other deeply, because love covers over a multitude of sins." Halleluiah! What would we do without this truth? This verse reminds me of the bandages and kisses I would give to my young children when they were injured while playing outside or in a ball game. While I couldn't cure every injury, I could cover the small ones to prevent infection and further damage. I gave kisses to my children to encourage them and help them return to the game.

> If we love our children to the best of our ability, much of our imperfect parenting will be covered by God's grace.

Thankfully, God can accomplish much more for our children through our simple acts. We cannot be sinless parents, but if we love our children to the best of our ability, much of our imperfect parenting and the damage it could cause will be covered by God's grace. God can take our mistakes and work them into His overriding plan of blessing for our kids. What a comforting truth. Even if we are too easy on our children in one area and too hard in another, God can cover the discrepancies with His grace. Even when difficulties squelch our positive feelings toward our kids, God can help us care for them in a way that will bless them. When we feel exhausted and cannot give any more, God can multiply the efforts we do make.

4. How do you think God feels about your uncertainties or inabilities to fix all of your child's problems?

_____

_____

_____

5. Do you feel it is your job to be certain about the way you respond in every situation concerning your child? If not, what is your job?

_____

_____

_____

6. What might this look like from day to day?

_____

_____

_____

Focusing on What Your Children Really Need

Of course, there are some things we cannot give our children even if we try. We can encourage and train, but we are ultimately not in control of our child's internal level of motivation, work ethic, calm spirit, courage, or perseverance. At a certain age, we cannot make friends for them, job interview for them, or make them take care of their own health. We cannot make them happy or give them faith in God. We can teach, train, and set an example, but we cannot control whether they will listen or follow our advice. Ultimately, our children will make their own decisions, face their own consequences, and decide for themselves what will rule their lives. As parents, this can be both scary and wonderful—scary because we have so little control, and wonderful because God has it all.

The reality is that we will never know for certain how to parent perfectly. We truly need to become content with seeking God's help and then doing our best with the particular skills He has given us. We all have different personalities as parents, and two parents with completely different styles can both produce good kids.

In our differences, however, it is still good to strive toward some overarching principles for loving and raising our children. Of course, the ultimate guide for loving others comes from definitions and examples in God's Word. We have already discussed sacrifice and long-suffering as elements of love, but I want to refer again to 1 Corinthians 13: 4-7. In this scripture, Paul tells us that "love is patient, love is kind," that "it does not envy, it does not boast, it is not proud," it is "not self-seeking, it is not easily angered," and that it "always trusts, always hopes, always perseveres." This biblical definition can serve as a foundation for us as we love our children to the best of our ability.

When I was in the trenches of parenting my children, I often took time to examine my own strengths and weaknesses in this role. As I researched principles of loving my children well, including 1 Corinthians 13, I found there are certain things my children need no matter what parenting techniques I use. I need to be reminded of these things frequently, so years ago I made the following list to help me:

Things My Children Really Need

1. *Unconditional Commitment:* My children need to know that I am committed to their welfare in good times and bad.
2. *Acceptance:* Even in my children's worst moments, they need me to accept them, love them, and claim them as my own.
3. *Praise:* My children need affirmation for the things they do well or right.
4. *Patience and Gentleness:* My children need me to act and speak in a kind and gentle manner. They need me to say what I mean without using harsh body language and rash or angry words.
5. *Respect for Needs and Wants:* My children may want different things than I value. They need me to honor these differences, within reason, depending on their age and abilities.
6. *Flexibility:* My children need me to be willing to try new things. They need me to release rigid ideas about how things must be done and modify traditions that do not work.
7. *Consistency:* My children need me to steadily reinforce our family's chosen core values.
8. *One-on-one Time:* My children need me to value them enough to set aside time for just them.
9. *Maintenance of Dignity:* My children need me to say and do nothing that will dishonor or humiliate them.
10. *Appreciation of True Self:* My children need me to appreciate them for who they are rather than some expectation I set up in my mind.

I discovered the items on my list through prayer, research, and my own personal reflection of experiences interacting with my children. The positive principles reflected *my personal* parenting challenges at the time I compiled the list, which reminded me to focus in these areas. Your list might look somewhat different. My list is not the official "good parenting list"—other important qualities for raising special-needs kids include keeping a sense of humor, knowing when to ask for help, having the ability to forgive, giving thanks for small blessings, and maintaining discipline. You will be able to develop your own list depending on your family's specific needs and dynamics.

Another list you might want to make can center around particular therapies or skills your child needs to move forward with his or her development. These items can weigh heavy on your mind—especially when your children are young—so listing them can help keep your thoughts in order. Note that this particular list will change over time as your children accomplish certain skills or you realize some of the goals you have set are out of your control. This was true of my list, and over time I learned to focus on goals that I could accomplish myself (such as setting up opportunities for my children to learn new skills), even if my children could not or did not cooperate with me.

7. What items would you add or delete from the list I gave of what your child needs from you as a parent? Make your own list to follow and/or share.

_____

_____

_____

Special Needs of Adolescents

Although children of all ages have certain needs in common, some special considerations need to be made for adolescents. Before I explain those needs, let me first comment on the good news regarding the teen years. First of all, you can enjoy your teenagers even if they have social, emotional, or behavioral challenges! I am living proof. Second, children generally experience refined brain connectivity in adolescence (approximately between the ages of twelve and twenty-four), so they will get a second chance to learn some life skills and principles they may have missed when they were younger. Please take heart in this. It means that parenting your teens may not be as scary as you expect.

No matter what the teen years look like in your family, I hope the following discussion will remind you of some well-accepted guidelines as you enter this phase of parenting. My purpose is not to give specific techniques for addressing problem behavior, but to clarify basic principles that apply to children with and without social, emotional, and behavioral challenges.

Freedom of Choice

As you likely know, adolescents need more freedom of choice than younger children. Even if their skills are limited, it is important to allow them to make choices from a list of options you give them. This can be a difficult transition if you kept tight control on your children when they were very young. For example, if you have a child with autism, you probably learned to push him or her into activities so he or she would try new things at an early age. While such an early intervention philosophy is great for young children, it is no longer as helpful once children reach adolescence and desire to choose more of their own preferences for their lives. You can still encourage and pass on parental wisdom to your children, but you need to slowly hand over more control.

As difficult as this transition can be for parents, it helps to remember that it is normal and developmentally important for adolescents to want more decision-making power. This is true for kids with special needs as well as for typical children. Failing to let your child make choices can lead to rebellious behavior or may stymie his/her ability to make independent decisions in the future. Of course, because your child has social, emotional, or behavioral challenges, it is possible that one of these outcomes will occur even if you do allow more control. There are no guarantees, but letting your kids take more control over their lives as they age is a good principle to follow in most situations.

Self-Esteem Issues

As parents, most of us can recall from our own teenage years how easily self-esteem can be rocked during adolescence. For children with social, emotional, or behavioral challenges, the assaults on self-worth are even more intense. Our kids may often feel as if they are falling short of expectations, and this makes it difficult for them to maintain a healthy self-esteem. Teens can be more self-critical than their parents imagine—even though they might not outwardly claim to feel badly about themselves. In response, as parents, we need to be increasingly aware of whether or not the demands we place upon our kids are realistic. Striving toward age-appropriate goals is great, but there are times that helping your adolescent maintain a healthy psychological state is more important than academic or social progress you had hoped to see.

Preparing for Adulthood

Even if you know the wisdom behind considering your child's choices and psychological health as he/she enters adolescence, it can still be difficult for you to witness delayed development or deferred goal achievement. Our society has prescribed certain ages for goal achievement, such as expecting kids to graduate from high school at age seventeen or eighteen. But what if the stresses of dealing with social, emotional, or behavioral challenges put your child behind the typical schedule for completing school or getting a job? Again, you need to remember that *it really is okay* for your family to adopt a more workable schedule if need be. There is no reason for us to keep walking on the "typical treadmill" if we just cannot maintain the pace. Thankfully, God did not decree any specific educational attainment or career timetable for His people, since He has much more important and eternal goals in mind. Yes, it is true that school and work achievements can be important in our society, but we have to learn to be realistic, flexible, and creative with our situation. Nobody really cares in the long run what year your child completed high school, and once K-12 school is left behind, there are more opportunities for your child to pursue areas of his/her interest and to forge a unique path. Flexible scheduling is more easily accomplished once our child's routine is not prescribed by the school system.

In concluding this section, I want to emphasize again that prayer, consulting with your child's doctor and/or therapist, talking with other parents, and following your own intuition can help you determine how to handle the teen years. Keep in mind that what you decide is good for your child will not necessarily be what other children with similar disabilities or challenges need. We need to constantly refrain from comparing our situations to one another, even in special-needs families, and to remember that each child and family is unique. What works in one family will not always work in another. Let's not let parental pride and comparison twist us into anxious knots over delayed or altered achievement.

No matter what your child needs, be confident that if you request it, God will equip you to do what is in His will for your child. In 2 Corinthians 9:8, Paul states, "God is able to make all grace abound to you, so that in all things at all times, having all that you need, you will abound in every good work." Parenting your child well is certainly a "good work," so be confident God will equip you and extend grace for the task.

Celebrating Moments

One of the most difficult times for parents of a special-needs child to remain positive and joyful is when they diligently try to help their child but see little progress. I have experienced this challenge many times. Just recently, I was feeling discouraged because my older daughter, Katie, is still looking for a permanent job. She has graduated from high school and secured a summer job, but she has not yet found a year-round job. I have tried to be patient, but I really do want to see her progress to this next milestone of young adulthood.

I'm also threatened by discouragement over the medical problems that affect my younger daughter, Madeline. They affect her energy and ability to participate in social activities and have left her somewhat isolated. Of course this concerns me. I am anxious to see her bounce back into an active social life closer to the one she once led.

As I was lamenting this slow progress and trying to figure out what to do next, a friend reminded me that we need to celebrate the *moments* of progress as well as the milestones.

> We need to celebrate the *moments* of progress as well as the milestones.

Finding happiness in the small things is good for our souls. It is also a good habit to teach our children. Milestones may take years to accomplish, and we simply need encouragement more often than that. We need to celebrate the positive moments.

A moment may include watching our child respond more calmly to discipline, even if it has only happened once so far. It may be some successful days our child had at school, even if he or she is still anxious about it. It may be that our child is smiling more often or playing better with a sibling. Our son may not have a meltdown when playing a board game, or our daughter may be able to sit through the singing at a church service. Whatever the moment, we need to celebrate it when progress occurs. As we do, we will find that some of these moments will happen more often and even turn into days of progressive achievement, while others will just remain isolated moments to celebrate. But we must embrace all of them, for they are precious and may be the best we have for a while. If we miss them, we miss out on real reasons to be happy.

In my own situation, I have since found opportunities to celebrate my children's positive moments. For instance, I celebrate the fact that Katie has become more competent and comfortable with the process of job procurement, which is an occupation in its own right. I also celebrate that she enjoys her summer job and her volunteer job. In Madeline's case, I celebrate that she was able to go to a sleepover recently with a group of long-time friends and have a great time. Her medical symptoms often interfere with participation in such outings, but this past weekend was successful. Instead of worrying about what symptoms may affect her next week, I took time to celebrate this joyous event.

In addition to remembering the moments as they occur, we also need to remember all the things our child has achieved in the past. Often we are so anxious for the next milestone that we overlook the academic, social, and behavioral progress our child has made during the past few years. We have to remind ourselves to focus on these achievements and on the happy moments when they happen, especially during difficult seasons of life. This is where the Evidence of Hope Record that we began in chapter 1 can be of great help. If you have not updated that list in a while, this is the time to look back at it, reflect on it, and add to it.

Principles and Actions of a Persevering Parent

There are other actions we can take to help us persevere with hope and joy as we walk through both positive and negative moments in our child's life. Here are some useful principles and practical actions that I have learned:

Principle	Associated Action
Principle 1: First think of your son or daughter as a *child*, and second as a child with *special needs*.	Look at baby pictures and list the joys your child has given you.
Principle 2: Never, ever, give up on your child.	Use babysitters or respite care to allow yourself regular breaks for rest and rejuvenation.
Principle 3: Acknowledge that some days will seem hopeless and overwhelming but that tomorrow is a new day with new possibilities.	Go to bed early so you can face tomorrow with new strength.
Principle 4: Know that your attitude will greatly affect your child's perception of his or her abilities and disabilities.	Take a close look at yourself, your values, and what you believe about your child.
Principle 5: Strive to have a balanced, realistic, and positive attitude and to avoid extreme statements and thoughts.	Talk to someone rational.
Principle 6: Strive to be intentional with your statements and interactions with your child.	Assess the problem, plan a strategy, and work the plan.
Principle 7: Save energy to be the spouse and/or parent you want to be, as these jobs are likely the most significant you will ever hold.	Do not over commit to activities that drain your energy—you are not replaceable.
Principle 8: Be patient, knowing that a steady diet of encouragement *slowly* shapes a person and that every action has the potential to build or damage.	Pray a lot, plan your responses to difficulty, and take regular breaks.
Principle 9: Expect to make mistakes and give yourself permission to learn and be imperfect.	Learn to apologize to others and to forgive yourself.
Principle 10: Believe in the principle of HAPPY: **H** Have faith in the eternal (see Isaiah 40:8) **A** Accept pain as real (see John 16:33) **P** Persist in bringing forth the good (see Colossians 3:2; Philippians 4:8) **P** Practice peace (see Isaiah 26:3; 2 Corinthians 10:5) **Y** Yelp for joy in your hope, for Jesus has overcome the world (see John 16:33)	Learn the HAPPY acronym!

8. What actions will you take to increase your chance of persevering through future challenges with your child?

_____

_____

_____

From the Mouths of Babes

As I prepared to write this chapter, I found myself wondering what children would identify as helpful things their parents do to help their child learn and grow. I asked parents of special-needs kids to ask this question of their child. I received several answers, but my favorite was from a five-year-old boy named Austin, who has autism. He said, "Mommy help me free me."

Austin's statement is precious and beautiful, and it perfectly sums up a great truth. Just as Jesus sets us free from our bondage to sin and death, Austin sees his mother as helping him break free of autism. And she is doing just that. Although autism holds Austin in a type of bondage and makes it difficult for him to function in the world, his mother works hard to free him from as many anxieties and sensory sensitivities as possible so he can better interact with others. More importantly she diligently teaches him about Jesus.

I know this five-year-old did not mean to impress his mother with his profound statement and that he does not understand the impact of his words, but I believe they were meant to encourage his mother and us. Even if we cannot fix everything for our children, the physical and spiritual efforts we make are invaluable. In those areas in which we cannot free our children, God can—and will—in His time. In Christ, our children have a bright future. This is a truth we *all* need to understand.

9. What do you do that helps your child the most? If possible, ask your child this question, and then write the answer below.

_____

_____

_____

_____

_____

10. What does this answer mean to you?

_____

_____

_____

Prayer Thought

Heavenly Father, the needs of my child are numerous and constant. I never feel as if I have "made it," or that I have come to the end of my striving. I know I must balance and prioritize what I do to aid my child and my family. Guide me, Lord, to know what my child needs from me each step of the way. Help me to discern the priorities and meet the needs; and when I cannot meet the needs, help me to be content in Your care and timing. In Jesus' name, Amen.

Chapter 10

LIVING HAPPILY EVER AFTER

We all hope for it—that is, to live the reality described in the title of this chapter. I know that the longing to see my family live a fairy-tale ending has been a strong motivation for me to persevere as a parent. I expect that you feel the same. Years ago, I bought a plaque that spoke to this life dream. It has scrolling letters that spell out, "And they lived happily ever after." It is beautiful in a whimsical, Snow-White sort of way, but I haven't yet hung it up. Why? Although I really like it, I'm not quite sure I believe it, so I can't bring myself to display it on the wall.

Even though I have not been able to fully embrace the words on the plaque, I have not given it away, but have it tucked away in a closet. I just have not been willing to give up the dream of a happy ending. Hope is powerful and God is good, because today as I write this chapter, I'm struck by a new sense of the spiritual truth and encouragement found in the statement on that plaque. In fact, I think I will hang it up after all. I'm saving some of the good news and encouragement regarding happy endings for the conclusion of this book. But for now, I want to begin by sharing a practical and fun technique that can help our families move toward that end.

Writing Your Own Happy Ending

We have already discussed how our child's uniqueness will determine the best techniques and approaches to help him or her. Similarly, the tools that will best help us cope as parents are also person-specific. The intent of this book has not been to review the latest research or suggest particular therapies, but there is one area of research that is so fascinating I would like to share it. This research demonstrates that to some degree, *people can write their own happy endings.*

Several studies have been completed over the years to illuminate how people overcome difficult circumstances.[19] Many reveal that people who can picture their future success are sometimes more likely to achieve it. This is especially true when people have high expectations for achieving their goal, when the goal is attainable, and when this thinking enhances a person's motivation and task performance. Imagining success also works best when people picture themselves performing well from a third-person perspective. For example, you are likely to have most success when you visualize yourself achieving your goal in story form—as if you were watching yourself respond to life challenges like an audience watches a movie.

In our families, the movie might look like something in the following scenario. You, the main character, are trying to be patient while helping your son with homework. In scene one, you are in the kitchen working on math problems with your youngster, who is fighting your every attempt to help. You work on one problem for thirty minutes. Finally, as you attempt to write down an example problem to show the steps, your son grabs the paper, crumples it up, and throws it across the room. In response, you yell at him and grab tightly onto his arm until it turns red. Then, in frustration, you throw your pencil across the room and move your child into position for a spanking. He struggles, and it turns into a scuffle that leaves both of you feeling angry and disrespected. Although your child needed some sort of correction, you regret not only that you did not handle the situation well, but also made it worse. You know the next homework situation will trigger a similar negative response, and you feel you have failed in your parenting.

This is where the first scene of the movie ends. Scene two is yet to be determined. Will you continue to react to your child in this way when these outbursts occur, or will things change? Here is the potential turning point where visualization comes into play. When you visualize a more helpful response, you can reverse your initial reaction. After your son throws the paper, you might take a deep breath and take a break. You may ask for help from your spouse or call a friend. You may decide to talk to your son's teacher or find a math tutor. You may calmly state a consequence for your child in response to his outburst without yelling at him, grabbing him, or throwing the pencil across the room.

If you visualize any of these more productive responses, it will be easier to play this part in real life. The natural consequence is that your happy ending is more likely to occur. Your child may still struggle with math, but you will have found a response or solution to the problem because you can visualize it. The technique is to choose a current parenting struggle and put it into story form, with you and your family members acting out the main characters. You can even start by picturing movie stars in your visualization if that sounds fun.

Another story might look like the following. Picture the camera on you as you deal with frustration over your sister's inability to see that your child's anxiety is due to an illness. She and other family members often accuse you of giving in to his childhood fears and causing the anxiety. In your heart, you know this is not true. Your child came into the world with a biochemical predisposition toward anxiety and you are doing your best to acknowledge his fears as you also teach him better coping skills. You have researched the problem and consulted with professionals, but your sister seems to think she has all the answers. You want to completely lose your cool and yell at someone. But you don't …

In the pivotal scene in this story, your character begins to turn from anger to understanding. Instead of yelling, you ask God for and listen to His wisdom. Somehow, the tension is transformed into peace. You are able to say just the right words to explain the truth to your sister without becoming angry. You are even able to listen to any helpful suggestions she might have. It is a beautiful scene, and it begins to heal the family discord. God helps you make this scene a reality. He brings to mind the outcome you want and shows you how to achieve it.

You can do this with any problem by simply asking God to give you a vision of a change that needs to take place and what that might look like. Imagine a situation, ask God for help, picture what your character does, and then put that into action when the situation occurs in real life. This is a technique that our children can also use to visualize their responses. It is likely something to which they can relate, especially since movies have such an influence on American life.

Of course, you cannot force the other actors in your movie to perform their parts according to your vision. People can still respond poorly to your attempts to problem solve. However, when *you* start to behave more like the courageous heroine or hero in your movie instead of a victim in a horror flick, the emotions often shift and others will learn to respond more appropriately. This "movie-making" process may sound silly, but it can work. I encourage you to try it and have fun with the process.

1. What does your first thought of "happily ever after" look like in your family?

_____

_____

_____

2. What sort of personal or family problem could you put into movie form to serve as a learning experience and technique for change?

_____

_____

_____

Living One Day at a Time

In our pursuit of happiness, the visualization or movie-making technique helps us by encouraging the development of new, more effective behaviors. It is also a lot more fun to implement than using sheer grit. Note that this is not a quick, one-time fix for happiness-depleting problems—it works scene by scene, one step at a time.

A one-day-at-a-time approach is also biblical. In Matthew 6:34, Jesus tells us not to worry about tomorrow's troubles. His actual words are, "Do not worry …" This sounds like a commandment, although I wonder how many of us have treated it as little more than an impossible suggestion. Until recently, this has been my interpretation, so it is no wonder that worry has been a struggle for me. Jesus intended for us to actually obey this command if we want to have a joyful life.

The complicating factor is that, of course, we do need to *think* about tomorrow, even if we do not worry about it. We have to make some plans for events in the near future, such as the upcoming school year, and we have to look far enough ahead to prepare our children for adulthood. Planning and working for a good future is also biblical (see Proverbs 6:6-8; 20:4; 31:14-16).

So how do we accomplish both of these seemingly incongruous tasks—taking things one day at a time *and* planning for the future? Most of us tend to lean toward the extreme—we are either planner/worriers or procrastinator/free spirits. The ability to master this mindset involves a God-given grace that does not come naturally to most of us. It can take a great amount of faith and obedience to prepare for the future without worrying about it. In the next section, we will highlight scriptures that can direct us to handle this issue.

Laughing at the Days to Come

Preparing for the future without worry goes against my instincts. I am a planner who wants to see the plan succeed, and I like to be in the driver's seat to make sure it happens. This is why passages such as Proverbs 31, which describes a woman who can "laugh at the days to come" (v. 25), used to be troublesome for me. This woman does not fear the days ahead but feels lighthearted about them. In contrast, I admit that I sometimes feel heavyhearted about the future. What is with this woman in Proverbs, anyway? I mean, clearly she didn't have a child with social, emotional, or behavioral challenges. If she did, it seems her story would be different.

For years the Proverbs 31 woman was a thorn in my side. She was supposed to inspire women to have good character, but mostly she caused me guilt and irritation. The Bible tells us "her lamp does not go out at night" (Proverbs 31:18). I thought that meant she was so energetic she hardly needed to sleep, which was hard for me, because I really needed my sleep. It also irked me that she "gets up while it is still dark" and "provides food for her family" (v. 15). I am happy if there is milk in the refrigerator and cereal in the cupboard. How was I ever to achieve her excellence?

Now when I look at Proverbs 31, I no longer interpret the details of this woman's life in such a literal way. I am able to see the bigger picture and realize her essence is about being a "wife of noble character ... worth far more than rubies" (v. 10). She provides for her family (v. 15), watches over the affairs of her household, and is not lazy or idle (v. 27). She works vigorously (v. 17), opens her arms to the poor and needy (v. 20), and prepares for the future (vv. 21-22). She speaks with wisdom, gives faithful instruction (v. 26), and serves God (v. 30). Her children and husband consider her a blessing (v. 28). These are wonderful qualities, and thankfully they have nothing to do with cooking from scratch or staying up all night.

One of my favorite portions of Proverbs 31 is verse 25, which says, "She is clothed with strength and dignity; she can laugh at the days to come." I also find it interesting that the two phrases in this verse are joined together by a semicolon. Writers use this particular punctuation when they want to suggest a relationship between two phrases without spelling it out for the reader. It allows a chance for the reader to think a bit about why the phrases are connected. In this particular verse, I think the connection suggests that this woman's ability to "laugh" has something to do with her strength and dignity. There is a lesson in this for us because it takes a lot of spiritual strength and God-given dignity for many of us to feel this good about the futures our families may face.

How do we gain this strength to face the future with a smile? First, we need to truly believe what God says to us through His Word and in answer to our prayers. Second, when we are tempted to worry, we are to "take captive every thought to make it obedient to Christ"(2 Corinthians 10:5). We are strengthened when we *do* this and don't just talk about doing it. It requires a moment-by-moment obedience that involves becoming aware of our thoughts, testing them for worry, and immediately choosing to replace these thoughts with God's promises.

For many years, this process of capturing our thoughts and replacing them has been utilized by professional counselors and therapists under a different name, known as "thought stopping." The key to this technique is to replace our negative or fearful thoughts with true, realistic, and positive ones. There is no better supply of such thoughts than in God's Word. Sometimes biblical thoughts may *seem* unrealistic because on earth we only see "a shadow of the good

135

things that are coming, not the realities themselves"(Hebrews 9:28). Hebrews 8:5 assures us that true eternal reality resides in the kingdom of heaven, and that earthly things are just a "copy and shadow of what is in heaven." Heavenly hope and thoughts may seem too good to be true because we have seen only a shadow of the gifts that await us in God's full presence in heaven. But, remember that Jesus told us that the kingdom of heaven became near (Matthew 4:17) with His fulfillment of God's promise of a savior. So heavenly promises are *not* too good to be true—they are just part of an eternal reality that we cannot yet fully understand.

> Heavenly promises are *not* too good to be true—they are just part of an eternal reality that we cannot yet fully understand.

Dignity seems to be the second attribute of the Proverbs 31 woman that promotes her ability to see the future with a positive outlook. Dignity originates from and contributes to a variety of positive experiences in a person's life. However, the most powerful contribution to our sense of dignity comes from knowing that we are children of God, and that our value remains the same regardless of time or circumstances. As a parent of a special-needs child, we do not need to be concerned with any future disgrace or honor we may receive as a result of how our child "turns out." The worth and dignity you, I, and our children carry were sealed when Jesus died on our behalf.

Although I am still struggling to win my war over worry, it has helped me to look deeply into the woman God described as an example. To not worry takes daily effort, but anxiety does not hinder my joy as it did years ago. This is not because there are no problems that threaten my family's future, but because I no longer fear them like I once did. I still prepare for future events, as the Proverbs 31 woman did (see vv. 21-22), but I am more lighthearted because I have confidence that God loves, honors, and provides in all circumstances. I have placed those concerns with the One who can handle them, so I can go about the business God created for *me*.

> We do not need to micromanage God's plans for our family's future: our job is to simply invest the talents He has given us.

In the parable of the talents, Jesus tells about the importance of doing the business God has given us (see Matthew 25:14-30). We do not need to micromanage God's plans for our family's future: our job is to simply invest the talents He has given us. He gave us tasks, and we receive joy when we use our talents to accomplish them. We have been created to give every effort to the work God gives us *today*, but not to worry about tomorrow. This is the key to laughing at the days to come.

3. What thoughts do you tend to have about your child's future and how this might affect your future as well?

_____

_____

_____

4. How can you plan ahead but also learn to laugh at the future?

_____

_____

_____

5. What are some specific steps you can take to make this more likely to happen?

_____

_____

_____

Letting Go

As much as we might hate to admit it, a time will come when we will no longer be able to fully plan our child's future and implement the plan. If our children have not yet taught us this lesson, most of us will experience it when they become young adults and no longer heed every piece of our good advice. Our plans may not succeed because our children are not capable or motivated to carry them out. Also, outside influences—such as friends, a job, or a living situation—may affect their decision making and/or execution of plans.

Age and time will also alter our plans for our children. As I age and my children reach young adulthood, I find I have less energy and drive to manipulate my children's circumstances. Sometimes I feel guilty that my involvement in my children's lives has declined—especially if I think a better outcome might have resulted had I intervened—while at other times I am thankful for the freedom this natural process has allowed. Even though it is normal and healthy to start letting go when children enter the late teen years, it can be a difficult transition.

While it can still be beneficial to be involved during our children's teen years, we need to be careful that we are not doing for them what they can do for themselves. Over-involvement can decrease our children's ability to grow and learn. Of course, it is often difficult to discern when our intervention will be helpful or harmful. Talking to other parents, a counselor, or other wise people can help us sort this out. Also, there is nothing like trial and error to teach us what works best to support our young adults.

Fear is a big reason why many of us are unable to allow our children to make decisions and suffer the consequences. Often, as parents of young adult children with social, emotional, or behavioral challenges, we worry about how they will react to the demands placed on them. We fear they might get hurt, drop out of school, run away, or harm themselves. We fear they could become teenage parents, drug abusers, homeless, or that they could just plain embarrass us. We fear that what our children do and what happens to them might be something they (and we) can't handle.

I understand how easy it is to be motivated by fear and to choose to intervene on behalf of our adolescent children to prevent harm. However, while fear is a part of being human, living in its grip is not God's will for us. Fear should not rule our decisions, paralyze us, or imprison us in living a life aimed only at preventing bad things from happening. Most of the things we fear never happen, so it is a feeling that is not always based in reality.

A big part of our ability to release the control over our children as they get older is to trust that God loves them more than we do. He also loves *us* and does not want our lives to be ruled by fear. Aside from fulfilling the role of mother or father to our children, we are *individually* important to Him, and He wants us to develop into the people He intended for us to become. Our personal health, interests, and relationships to other people matter as well.

The condensed version of this discussion is that it really is okay to let go of control over your children. Ask God to retrain you to care about your children and be supportive without trying to solve each and every problem. No matter what happens refuse to succumb to fear or despair. Years ago when I found myself fearing for my children's future, I would remember Psalm 16:8, which states, "I have set the LORD always before me. Because he is at my right hand, I will not be shaken." When I became fearful, I would focus on my right hand to remember this verse when I needed it the most. These words reminded (and still remind) me that the Lord is as close as my right hand and that I do not need to live in fear, because He is always there.

Let go of the control. Do not fear or despair, but declare the truth of Psalms 16:8. Declare it out loud and as often as you need. God has you and your children by the hand.

6. What part does fear play in how you raise your children? How can you raise your children in a way that is not based in fear?

_____

_____

_____

Dysfunction Junction

If we find we cannot let go of control over our children as they become young adults and/or we feel guilty for wanting to take care of our own needs, it may be that we have become entangled in a dysfunctional relationship within the family. Maintaining a functional family requires a balance of giving support, sharing responsibility, and establishing rules, boundaries, and discipline. It is more likely for this balance to get off-kilter if someone in the family has social, emotional, or behavioral challenges.

Marriage and family therapist and author Karla Downing says that dysfunction is found in families who lack productive communication and conflict-resolution skills.[20] These families can sometimes be identified because they tend to fight the same battles over and over again with no resolution. Another sign of dysfunction is when one member of the family is constantly picking up the pieces for an irresponsible member.

Because part of raising children with special needs is giving extra support when needed, it takes wisdom to discern when we are actually giving too much support and picking up too many pieces. If we see any of these signs in our family, or if we begin to wonder if we are giving too much support, it is time to seek counseling from a wise friend or professional. A good resource for learning how to keep family life balanced while living with a difficult person is Downing's book _When Love Hurts: 10 Principles to Transform Difficult Relationships._ This book applies primarily to relationships between adults, but it is also applicable to parents who have teens or young adult children.

7. Do you see any signs of dysfunction in your family, especially as it relates to your child as an adolescent or young adult?

_____

_____

_____

8. If so, what help can you seek to find a more positive balance?

_____

_____

_____

Living Happily Ever After

As discussed in the contents of this book, my tendency in special-needs parenting has been to fear that villains or circumstances would upset my earthly happily-ever-after story. Maybe you can relate to this fear. As a young mother, I thought I believed in God's promise that I did not need to fear. However, the uncertain outcomes of parenting still triggered my anxiety. I was constantly looking for some formula that would assure my children's success and give me unshakeable peace of mind.

Years ago I attended a Christian ladies' luncheon. The speaker for the event was a woman named Leah. She appeared to have a picture-perfect Christian life, but then she shared the heartbreaking story of her prodigal son. This wayward child had left a loving home at the age of sixteen to live on the drug-ridden streets of San Francisco. As a young mother I could hardly imagine anything worse. As Leah continued to share, I was somewhat comforted to learn that her son had returned home several years later and cleaned himself up. His next move, however, was to father a child out of wedlock. Walking through the pain of her son's life almost caused Leah to become suicidal. She had worked so hard to have a perfect life, but it had been shattered. It was only through Christ that she received the strength to live past the pain.

After her message, the master of ceremonies mentioned there was another happy ending to the story, but she didn't tell the audience what it was. I was disappointed to miss it, because I desperately wanted to know that God created happy endings. Weeks later, I happened to be in Leah's business office for an unrelated purpose, so I gathered my courage and asked about that happy ending. She told me that while her son did not marry the mother of his child, her grandchild was a blessing. She also said her son had been a good father to her grandchild, even though he only saw his daughter a few days each week. It was not the picture-perfect ending I wanted to hear. Of course, nothing on earth could undo the situation or change any of her son's previous actions. There were consequences. However, I had forgotten one part of Leah's story.

Before she shared the story of her son, Leah had related how her father had abandoned her family when she was just a toddler. She never knew her father, and she grew up in physical and spiritual poverty as a result. The consequences of this situation plagued her childhood and crept into her adult life. She became very controlling in an effort to prevent more bad things from happening. Clearly, her son's actions did not work into her plans for a perfect family. However, for Leah, the fact that her son eventually became a loving father and did not abandon *his* family *was* a happy ending to her story. The cycle of absent fatherhood had been broken. God did not give her the perfect family on earth that she desired, but He gave her peace in the midst of the imperfection.

I have thought about Leah's story over the years. It did not have the fairy-tale ending she and I hoped for, but it was a *redeemed* ending. Some definitions of redeem are "to free from captivity by payment of ransom, to free from what distresses or harms, to change for the better, restore, repair, to make worthwhile, to convert into something of value."[21] This is exactly what happened in Leah's life and in the life of her son. God freed them from distress and harm and changed the pain into something of value!

Yes the pain still happened. The result of sin in the world means that illness, pain, and suffering will occur, and we cannot erase the hurts our children have felt or inflicted on others as a result of their pain. Nor can we completely prevent them from being wounded again in the future. We cannot erase anybody's sin or pain, but God can redeem it! With His help, our pain becomes valuable. It reminds us to be thankful for His guidance and comfort here on earth and helps us look forward to the day when we will be lifted up into His eternal presence. We all have the chance to enter into a relationship with God, but not all of us recognize its value. We need to take our chance, recognize it, and claim it!

> We cannot erase anybody's sin or pain, but God can redeem it. He can restore the loss and convert it into something of value.

Christ brings us full circle. God created us for paradise, and because of this we long for the happiness He intended. But because sin and illness touch our world, we grieve and sometimes despair. We try to call happiness and contentment into our lives, but we cannot do it in our own strength. Our only chance is to reach out to God the Father, the maker of heaven and earth, who created paradise for us. Although Adam and Eve rebelled against God's will for them, we can accept it with gladness. Although sin forced us into a yoke of slavery, we can choose a new direction in our relationship with Christ. Jesus instructed, "Take my yoke upon you and learn from me, for I am gentle and humble in heart, and you will find rest for your souls. For my yoke is easy and my burden is light" (Matthew 11:29-30). When we promise deference to God, He in return carries our burdens of pain and strife.

Part of the curse of the fall from grace in Eden was that humans were given toil all the days of their lives (Genesis 3:16-18). We still toil, but Christ offers to take the burden of that toil away from us. When we accept His gift, He eases the burden so that each day we can have a new beginning. Our energy is renewed (Psalm 103:5), and we can say with confidence, "I will dwell in the house of the LORD forever" (Psalm 23:6). We know this is true because we can experience some of God's heavenly peace here on earth. God gives us this happy ending—His redemption and His peace.

9. What is the meaning of "redemption" as outlined in the dictionary?

    _____

    _____

    _____

10. What is one way God might redeem the pain in your life or your child's life for something worthwhile?

    _____

    _____

    _____

11. Have you ever experienced a peace and joy that surpassed your understanding in the midst of your circumstances—a bit of heaven here on earth? If so, write a few notes about that experience.

    _____

    _____

    _____

A Name Change

As I conclude of this book, it is interesting to look back twenty years to the joyous day when my first daughter was born—and to how quickly that day led to my first experiences with special-needs parenting. This book outlines the quest for happiness and wholeness within that experience. I still pray for happiness for my children and family, and I am sure you share a similar desire. However, as I shared in the introduction to this book, my greater prayer is for God to affect my children profoundly and even rename them as He did with some of the men and women we know from Scripture.

Sometimes God renamed a person to reflect a character change or to indicate their submission to God, such as when Jacob (meaning "he deceives") became Israel ("one who struggled with God"; see Genesis 32:27-29). Sometimes He changed it to reflect a person's destiny, as when He changed Abram ("exalted father") to Abraham ("father of many"; Genesis 17:5). In Revelation 2:17, we read that at the end of time, the victorious in Christ will receive "a white stone with a new name written on it, known only to him who receives it." It is amazing to me that God knows each of us so intimately that He will rename us in a way so personally meaningful and significant that nobody else will know the name. I look forward to that day, but I also know God is happy for the changes He makes in us even now on earth.

While I am interested to see how God will impact my children, what I did not anticipate during the process of my child-rearing journey is how much He would change me. He took a somewhat prideful, self-sufficient young woman and allowed her to become scared, hopeless, and overwhelmed. He then pulled me out of that pit and put my feet on solid ground. He transformed me into someone who seeks Him. Life is still difficult, but it is not overwhelming because God walks with me and my children through everything. He has redeemed my life, and He is redeeming the lives of my children. He is able to restore all that has been lost as a result of social, emotional, or behavioral challenges. Hebrews 10:35-36 reminds us to boldly rely on this redemption: "So do not throw away your confidence; it will be richly rewarded. You need to persevere so that when you have done the will of God you will receive what He has promised." He is faithful. He is enough. I can persevere as a parent because I can laugh at the days to come. I hope you will join me.

> "So do not throw away your confidence; it will be richly rewarded. You need to persevere so that when you have done the will of God you will receive what He has promised."

12. What steps can you take right now to invite the joy and peace of God into your life?

_____

_____

_____

_____

Prayer Thought

God, I thank You for giving Your own Son to save me. I thank You for giving purpose and meaning to my experiences in this world. Help me to discover the new name You would give to me as I mature in Your love and grow in Your grace. I also ask this for my children and family, and I pray that they will recognize the personal knowledge and individual love You have for them. Please keep us in Your tender care. Amen.

APPENDIX: SUGGESTIONS FOR PERSEVERING PARENT SUPPORT GROUPS

The ideal size for a Persevering Parent Support Group is ten to fifteen parents, though a larger or smaller group should also work well. Experience suggests that the best length for each meeting is ninety minutes. This time frame will keep the class fresh and not overly long, and it will allow parents to spend about two hours away from home (assuming a fifteen-minute travel time to and from the class). This will ensure that the class is helpful to participants and not a burden due to an excessive time commitment.

Before the meeting date, each person should read a chapter in the book that will be discussed during the class time and write their answers in the spaces provided. I suggest taking forty-five to sixty minutes in class each week to discuss participant answers to questions. In a moderate-sized group, this amount of time is sufficient to discuss the contents of a chapter and allow the participants to share their answers to the questions. Any longer than this usually means that members are sharing long personal stories or that the class is getting off topic. Although it is good for participants to share their stories and move off topic to some degree, others may feel frustrated if this discussion time goes on and on.

To keep within the ninety minute time frame, try to limit the discussion on each question to between two and five minutes. To do this, it is helpful for the group facilitator to make notes in the margin next to each question to indicate at approximately what time the class should be done answering it. For example, if the class starts at 6:30, the first question in the chapter should be answered by 6:33, and the next question should be answered by 6:37, etc. If the facilitator adheres to this process throughout the class, it should move at a nice pace—not too hurried and not too slow.

I suggest using the next thirty to forty minutes to let each parent to share the high and low points of what is going on in their homes and hearts, to ask for prayer, and to share encouraging events from their Evidence of Hope Record. It is helpful to designate how much time each person can share—again just to make sure everyone has a chance to speak. Of course, this timing will depend on how many participants are in the group and how much time is left in your meeting. There will be times when one family or participant may be struggling more than others and will need to share more than their allotted time. Handling this will be up to the facilitator of the class, but usually letting that person take up a bit more time works because somebody else in the class may not have much to say that week. Finally, the remaining part of class can be used to pray.

My suggestion would be to either conduct the class once a week for ten sequential weeks (reading and discussing one chapter each week), or once every two weeks, over a period of twenty weeks. This decision should be left up to the group to suit the needs of the class. There is no right or wrong way to do this so feel free to make up a schedule that works for you—even meeting once per month would probably work.

These are suggestions based on my experience in using this book to lead a support group, but each class can be creative in how they structure the time and use the material. Another good way to encourage meaningful dialogue is to ask class participants which concepts in the week's lesson were most meaningful and applicable to their lives. If this question is asked at the end of the class, when members are giving their prayer requests, they can also indicate what change they are planning to make as a result of reviewing the content in the book for that week. This might promote meaningful thought or behavior change for those who want or need it.

Enjoy your group. Share, laugh, and cry together! You will likely find that the relationships you form within your Persevering Parent Support Group will be part of God's provision for strength while you walk through your parenting process.

REFERENCES

Chambers, Oswald. Edited by James Reimann. *My Utmost for His Highest.* Updated Edition. Grand Rapids: Discovery House Publishers, 1992.

De Vinck, Christopher. *The Power of the Powerless.* Doubleday, New York, 1988.

Dillow, Linda. *Calm My Anxious Heart: A Woman's Guide to Finding Contentment.* Colorado Springs: NavPress, 1998.

Downing, Karla. *When Love Hurts: 10 Principles to Transform Difficult Relationships.* Kansas City: Beacon Hill Press, 2004.

Johnston, Jon. *Christian Excellence: Alternative to Success.* Grand Rapids: Baker Book House, 1985.

Stanford, Matthew S. *Grace for the Afflicted: A Clinical and Biblical Perspective on Mental Illness.* Downers Grove, IL: InterVarsity Press, 2008.

Tada, Joni Eareckson, and Steven Estes. *When God Weeps: Why Our Sufferings Matter to the Almighty.* Grand Rapids: Zondervan, 1997.

Thomas, Gary. *Sacred Parenting: How Raising Children Shapes Our Souls.* Grand Rapids: Zondervan, 2004.

ENDNOTES

Chapter 1: Got Hope?

1. Douglas Moes et al., "Stress Profiles for Mothers and Fathers of Children with Autism," *Psychological Reports*, 71 (1992): 1272-1274; M.B. Olsson and C.P. Hwang, "Depression in Mothers and Fathers of Children with Intellectual Disability," *Journal of Intellectual Disability Research*, 45 (2001): 535-543.
2. *Merriam-Webster's Dictionary*, s.v. "hope," accessed Aug 2, 2013, http://www.merriam-webster.com/dictionary/hope.

Chapter 2: Living Your New Normal

3. "How Many People Have Disabilities?" Centers for Disease Control and Prevention, accessed July 18, 2013, http://www.cdc.gov/ncbddd/documents/Disability tip sheet_PHPa_1.pdf.
4. "Any Disorder Among Children," National Institute of Mental Health, accessed July 17, 2013, http://www.nimh.nih.gov/statistics/1ANYDIS_CHILD.shtml.
5. *Merriam-Webster's Dictionary*, s.v. "normal," accessed August 2, 2013, http://www.merriam-webster.com/dictionary/normal.
6. "Marriage and Divorce," American Psychological Association, accessed July 20, 2013, http://www.apa.org/topics/divorce/index.aspx.
7. Christopher de Vinck, *The Power of the Powerless* (New York: Doubleday, 1988): 14, 40.

Chapter 5: The Real Insanity: Stigma, Shame, and Silence

8. Reader's Digest Complete Word Finder, s.v. "stigma," (NY: Oxford University Press, 1996).

9. Catherine G. McLaughlin, "Delays in Treatment for Mental Disorders and Health Insurance Coverage," *Health Services Research* 39, no. 2 (2004): 221-224, http://www.ncbi.nlm.nih.gov/pmc/articles/PMC1361004.

10. Manoj J. Waikar (presentation, National Alliance on Mental Illness, California Chapter, San Francisco, CA, 2010).

Chapter 6: Attitude Check: The Power of Parents Living the Truth

11. Stacie Cockrell, interview by Mary Lou Aguirre, "What's Real Parenthood Like? Listen up," *The Fresno Bee,* Jan. 16, 2007.

12. Gary Thomas, *Sacred Parenting* (Grand Rapids: Zondervan, 2004): 11-21.

13. Hugh F. Johnston, "Caring for the Challenging Child: Everyday Management Techniques" (presentation, Foster and Kinship Care program, Redding, CA, 2004).

14. Edward T. Hall, *The Dance of Life* (New York: Doubleday, 1983), referred to in Roberta M. Berns, *Child, Family, School, Community: Socialization and Support,* 8th ed. (Belmont, CA: Wadsworth/Cengage Learning, 2009).

15. Oswald Chambers, *My Utmost for His Highest,* ed. James Reimann, Updated Edition (Grand Rapids: Discovery House Publishers, 1992): February 9.

Chapter 7: When You Get Ugly: Help for Parents Behaving Badly

16. "Any Disorder Among Children," National Institute of Mental Health, accessed July 17, 2013, http://www.nimh.nih.gov/statistics/1ANYDIS_CHILD.shtml.

17. Kathleen Ries Merikangas et al., "Prevalence and Treatment of Mental Disorders Among US Children in the 2001–2004 NHANES," *Pediatrics* 125, no. 1 (2010): 75-81, doi: 10.1542/peds.2008-2598.

Chapter 8: What About Me? Finding Abundance in Sacrifice

18. Jon Johnston, *Christian Excellence: Alternative to Success* (Grand Rapids: Baker Book House, 1985): 33.

Chapter 10: Living Happily Ever After

19. Noelia A. Vasquez and Roger Buehler, "Seeing Future Success: Does Imagery Perspective Influence Achievement Motivation?" *Personality and Social Psychology Bulletin* 3, no. 10 (2007): 1392-1405.

20. Karla Downing, *When Love Hurts: 10 Principles to Transform Difficult Relationships* (Kansas City: Beacon Hill Press, 2004): 32-34.

21. *Webster's New Collegiate Dictionary,* s.v. "redeem," (Phillipines: G. and C. Mirriam Company, 1981).

Dear Parent or Caregiver,

If you have perused or are reading this book, you are in my prayers. I would love to hear how Persevering Parent has worked for you as an individual or within your support groups. Please direct comments, questions or suggestions to me via my contact page at www.PerseveringParent.com.

Karen

26374444R00098

Made in the USA
San Bernardino, CA
27 November 2015